The Complete Guide To Beef Cattle Farming

Look Inside To Discover How To Become A Beef Cattle Farmer

Written by
Morris Halliburton

"Don't be afraid to take a big step if one is indicated. You can't cross a chasm in two small jumps."
David Lloyd George

Introduction

If you own and/or happen to be living on a few acres you may have the resources to raise a few beef cattle. Small beef cattle farms and ranches are becoming popular as a means to supplement off farm income.

Beef production is a large and important segment of American agriculture and one of the largest industries in the world. Beef enterprises work well with grain, orchard, vegetable, or other crop operations. Cattle can make efficient use of feed resources that have little alternative use, such as crop residues, marginal cropland, untillable land, or rangeland that cannot produce crops other than grass.

For people who own land but work full-time off the farm, a beef enterprise can be the least labor-intensive way to utilize their land. A cattle enterprise can use family or surplus labor. Calving, weaning, vaccinations, castration, and weighing can be planned for times when labor is available.

Consider your resources, the land available, and your level of interest before deciding to engage in the cattle business. Identify why you want to raise cattle and set goals to achieve the most constant economic return or personal satisfaction. Your goals must be clearly defined, firmly fixed, achievable, and have a realistic time frame. Otherwise, your operation will lack meaning, objective, and focus.

Raising a small beef cattle herd can be a very rewarding experience. Have you dreamed of living in the country but never figured out a least labor intensive enterprise to supplement your off farm income. One big advantage that most individuals discover is that such an enterprise is a great help towards many tax savings. However you should check with your personal tax advisor to determine your best advantages.

Listed below are a few different cattle related enterprises to consider. It is always best to do a thorough study to determine the most appropriate enterprise for your situation. And keep in mind that the best situation may be to use a combination of more than one enterprise when possible. Resource considerations may play a big part in your decision.

Registered or Seedstock Cow calf enterprise

Keeping a few high quality registered mother cows and raising calves from them. You would also need a good herd bull or breed your cows by artificial insemination. More record keeping and added value is needed in this kind of an operation but with a higher monetary return. Most everything needs to be recorded for performance records; the calves need to be weighed at birth and weaned and weighed at about 6 months of age. Learn More

Commercial Cow calf enterprise:

Keeping a few mother cows and raising calves from them. The calves normally would be weaned at about 6 months of age and weigh approximately 500 pounds.

Bottle calf beef enterprise

This is a labor intensive enterprise comprised of purchasing new born calves, usually a dairy breed and raising them until they weigh 300 to 500 pounds.

Feeder or stocker calf enterprise

Purchasing calves that weigh between 400 and 500 pounds and feeding them until they weigh from 700 to 900 pounds. Usually placed on pasture or on diets high in forage.

Market beef enterprise

Purchasing 700 to 900 pound calves and feeding them to market weight of 1100 to 1200 pounds. This can be very rewarding if you are close to a metropolitan population and sell direct to the consumer.

Purchasing Considerations

In most situations frame and conformation are more important than breed in relation to cattle performance. However, there are many things to consider.

Conclusion

Those interested in growing and raising beef cattle on their acreage can find it very rewarding. However it is recommended that one should first become knowledgeable and informed about the enterprise so that you do not become involved in an unmanageable and costly situation. Consult with feed company personnel, Extension staff, local veterinarians and local beef producers. Raising beef cattle can improve quality of life and provide great satisfaction and responsibility for families.

Success of your beef cattle enterprise depends on adapting a strategy that fits your needs. After generating some ideas about what kind of operation you would like to have, contact your Extension agent and work out a detailed plan.

This book gives an overview of the basics for developing and managing a small beef herd. The Extension Service, veterinarians, and experienced beef producers can be resources to help you develop your enterprise. Careful planning, quality cattle in good health, and good management will put you on the road to success.

It is my sincere wish that this short introduction has created many questions in your mind and that you will find all of your answers in the book.

Contents

Beef Cattle Farming Today

Beef cattle farming is a business that continues to grow around the world. There is definitely a demand for quality meat out there. Some of these farms have been in families for generations. They proudly pass down their land and their knowledge in order to be a part of it all. For others though, the idea of beef cattle farming is something they are brand new to.

It may be a desire to make money, as there is plenty of it found when you raise quality cattle and then sell them for the meat. Many individuals just want to get away from the city and a hectic lifestyle. They find the country air refreshing and raising cattle to be a way for them to make a decent living.

There is plenty that goes on behind the scenes though when it comes to beef cattle farming. You don't just turn the cows loose on your land, fatten them up, and then sell them for a profit. Learning more about what goes on with beef cattle farming can help you to decide if you should pursue it or not. It can also give the general public a good idea of why beef prices can change so often.

Raising quality cattle is vital to the success of such farming methods. The need to have more cattle is also there. This is why there are plans in place to get breeding done as effectively as possible. The males with the best genetic qualities are the ones allowed to mate with the females. The goal is to have at least one calf per female per season. Therefore, properly managing the heifers is part of the basis for making this work.

A combination of natural reproduction and artificial insemination is used in beef cattle farming. Thanks to the technology we have today, we don't have to rely solely upon nature to get the job done. Using a variety of tools, heifers can be successfully impregnated with the sperm of the bulls without the two being in contact with each other.

Offering quality land and feed for the cattle is important to their overall development. The females will have healthier offspring when their own needs are met. In turn, the young will grow up to be healthy and to have their own quality offspring. The meat from well fed cattle is better and so there is a higher profit earned from them.

When reproduction is well managed, the farmer won't

have to spend profits to purchase replacement heifers. Yet that doesn't mean there aren't any expenses to cover. For example there is the cost of all the feed that the cattle will need for survival. Supplements can also be expensive but today they are a common part of the process.

There is also the cost of routine care for the young cattle. Vaccinations can ensure they remain healthy. It can also prevent the spread of viruses that can kill large amounts of cattle. Should that occur, the financial security for a beef cattle farmer can be on shaky ground. Combination vaccines should be used when possible to cut down on costs. It will also cut down on the amount of time it takes for the young cattle to get immunized.

In the past, reducing nursing time for the young has occurred on beef cattle farms. However, studies show that this causes stress for the young. It can result in them not growing as large as they should during the first two years of life. The risk of serious health problems also increases.

Should nature be the determining factor when it comes to the birth of calves? Many farmers believe it is acceptable to intervene and to lend a hand when a heifer is having difficulties on her own. This may end up saving the life of both the mother and her young offspring.

More often, it is the first time mothers that need the most assistance with giving birth. The labor can last two or three times longer for them. However, complications can arise with any calf birth even if they have been successful with doing it on their own many times in the past.

Any time that a young calf is being born tail first, there is a need for intervention. This process is one that not everyone has the skills for so a vet may need to be called to the scene. There is limited time to help the calf in such a situation so you need to be able to make quick decisions. What happens is that the calf will start to come out backwards. This process puts pressure on the umbilical cord as it does do.

Then there is a limited supply of blood going from the mother to the calf. This can result in death or serious brain injury. The calf can also be in the birth canal with fluids around the mouth and nose. They can drown in them if they aren't taken out of the mother immediately. The calf has to be taken out of the body in under 4 minutes though if there is a chance of it surviving once the blood supply from the umbilical cord has been cut off.

The young calves will have to be further evaluated. Those that are doing well with their mothers should be left alone other than for checkups and when it is time for vaccinations. Those that are born underweight or that don't seem to be growing properly may need more one on one care from humans. The goal is to ensure all of the cattle are very healthy regardless of their age.

Yet it is especially necessary for the young so that serious health problems can be eliminated. If the calf can't grow to be big and strong it won't be very good quality of meat. If the calf is female, it may have a very difficult time giving birth when it is fully mature. Every effort should be taken to help pave the way for a healthy life from the very start for all of the cattle.

What is also interesting is that a difficult birthing experience for a heifer can result in her being less likely to become pregnant in the future. Since you do want all of the females in the herd that are mature to have a calf annually, helping with the birthing process can increase the chances of that happening. There are tools available that can be used to help the calf be born without causing additional stress to the mother.

Studies show that to prevent calves from being born at night, offer food at that time to the heifers. How this works isn't really known, but there is enough research out there to indicate it does result in fewer calves being born at night. Since supervision during the calving season is likely to take place during the day, you can reduce mortality rates with this simple but effective trick. Starting this process of night feeding 2 or 3 weeks before calving is to start is a good idea.

The young calves are the future for any beef cattle farm. It is important to document the number of births and the number of deaths that occur. Look for patterns if you have high mortality rates. You need to be able to find those contributing factors so that they can be reduced or eliminated before the following calving season. The problem could be with the bulls used for mating, the food sources, vaccines, a virus found on the land where they are at, and even the weather.

By documenting as much information as you can, you can find those links that result in the calves not surviving. The goal should be to see as many of them growing rapidly and gaining weight consistently. If that isn't happening with almost all of the calves then there is a serious situation that needs to be reviewed further.

While a great deal of attention is spent focusing on the calves and the heifers, the bulls also need quality care. They are the males that offer the sperm for the young calves to be created. Genetic testing of these animals is a good idea if you are going to use them to breed a large number of heifers. Ensuring that the bulls aren't genetically linked to serious health problems is important. Otherwise future generations of cattle can end up with those same genetic problems.

Bulls need a quality diet in order to grow like they should and to produce enough sperm for the mating season. It is a good idea to keep young bulls away from the older and more experienced bulls. Otherwise it often will reduce the rate of their growth. It will also cause them to become fully mature later than they normally would.

A diet that is carefully balanced for the needs of each bull is very important. Grain is a huge part of their diet and ensuring they make the right gains. On average, the bulls need to gain 2 pounds a day after they are weaned. This should continue until they are about 1,000 pounds. Monitoring growth will help to determine if the diet plan is working or if it needs to be modified.

With the technology available for artificial insemination it is now possible to impregnate a large number of heifers with only a handful of bulls. This is a very cost effective part of successful beef cattle farming. Many agree that the overall quality of the genetics from the males is more important than the number of them available. The number of bulls to have on a beef cattle farm is a personal decision though.

Other than breeding season, it is important to keep the bulls away from the heifers. They should be separated by pens with no chance of being able to come into contact with each other. The use of a high voltage electrical fence may be necessary to give a strong message that they are to remain separated. Bulls can be very powerful and aggressive so you must teach them where they are to remain.

The ongoing health of the bulls is just as important during the non breeding season as when they are mating. They need to have a quality diet, room to graze, and regular checkups. This will ensure they are ready to go at the peak of their game for the next mating season.

Adequate food for the other cattle is very important to evaluate too. Today many cattle farmers understand the importance of protecting their land. If the cattle consume it too close to the roots then the land may be useless in the future for grazing. This is why they often have sections in place. By rotating the areas where the cattle can graze, they give each area enough time to rejuvenate. Then the farmer can continue to use that land for grazing at different points in time.

There are plenty of different growth strategies that a beef cattle farmer can implement. Having a great strategy in place is important because that is what will determine the quality of the cattle. It will also determine the longevity of the operation. Therefore the big picture needs to be evaluated – not just right now and how to make the most money in the market right now.

The analysis of different types of feed need to be carefully reviewed. The type of environment where the cattle are grazing is part of the determining factors as well. Supplements can be used to help the heifers gain weight and to get the right balance of nutrition. Yet supplements can be very expensive so beef cattle farmers want to use them only when necessary. Otherwise they are cutting deeply into their profits.

Nature has a way of throwing things off course, so a beef cattle farm has to be ready for them. When there is too much heat and a drought sets in there may not be enough food on the land. Then more supplements have to be offered in order to keep the herd healthy. Additional water needs to be in place too so that they can survive. The extra heat can reduce the chances of pregnancy for the heifers. It can also reduce the strength and the size of the young calves.

The size of the herd of cattle on a farm is another very important issue to take into consideration. Of course the available space for grazing and living quarters needs to be taken into consideration. There are areas where these animals are packed too closely together and they should have some breathing room. That will reduce their stress and help them to be very healthy animals.

It is perfectly understandable that cattle farmers will increase the number of the herd when prices for beef are high. This is a great method for making more money and keeping profits high. It can help them to have some funding put away for business expenses or when they have a bad season. There are many highs and lows with the beef cattle industry so being prepared is important.

When beef prices are low, it can be more cost effective for a cattle farmer to reduce the number in the herd. That way the cost of feed and other related expenses is less. They can tighten their belts and at least break even when they do sell their cattle for beef. When you are involved with this type of business, you have to stay focused on what is going on out there.

Many beef cattle farmers find it is easier for them if they just remain consistent with their herd number. They feel it will all balance out in the end – some years they will make lots of money, others they will make a little bit. They will see years when they break even and also some when they have spent more than they earned. Yet they are confident with proper management they will be successful in the long run.

What is interesting though when you analyze data regarding cattle. You will notice that at the beginning and ending points of decade markers, the prices are higher. However, in the middle of the decades they seem to drop quite significantly. This type of pattern can help cattle farmers to make decisions based on what is likely to occur with pricing in the future as well.

When you have a herd of cattle, there are issues with health that need to be addressed. Should the cattle become ill, whatever is causing the problem could spread like a wildfire. It can be very expensive to take care of a large number of sick cattle. The illness may affect their ability to successfully breed in the future. In many instances, the illness may result in the death of a significant number of the cattle.

As I mentioned, proper vaccinations are important when

it comes to healthy cattle. While the cost of offering them can add up, you are walking a dangerous line if you have a beef cattle farm and your animals aren't vaccinated. That is the case with organic farm animals and it is why the meat is so expensive. They have a higher mortality rate and need to sell for a much higher amount than regular commercial cattle in order for the beef cattle farmers to make their money back.

The government of the United States isn't leaving it up to chance when it comes to viruses in the beef cattle industry. They have guidelines in place that need to be followed. This is why there are restrictions against imported cattle. That is also why they have feeding controls in place. The goal is to ensure the cattle are well cared for and that the people that will consume them aren't at risk.

An emergency plan of action should be in place in case you end up with sick cattle. They should be separated from those that are healthy. The isolation will help to prevent more from becoming ill. Keep in mind that with some types of viruses there are incubation periods. This means some cattle may not show symptoms of illness yet but they are going to in a few days. Careful observation is essential to keep the problem from getting out of control.

There is no denying that the beef cattle farming industry is one that we rely on for a variety of needs. Most people around the world do eat beef that comes from cattle. To keep up with the demand, new methods of raising cattle so that the meat is delicious are introduced. At the same time, the goal is to raise production and to cut overhead expenses.

The world of beef cattle farming has certainly changed over the course of time. It will be interesting to see what develops relating to it in the future. One thing is for certain though – consuming beef is going to continue. With policies in place for proper raising of the animals and safe processing there is less of a risk involved with consuming meat than in the past.

There are some ethical issues that will always surround beef cattle farming. You do have those that refuse to eat foods that come from animals. They don't feel it is right to raise cattle for the production of meat. They also don't agree with the methods that are used to fatten up the cattle. Yet there are enough people out there willing to overlook those issues in order to have the meat they love to eat.

For beef cattle farmers, it is a way of life that they are fine tuning. They want to get the most out of their efforts. Being able to make money while living off the land and raising animals is very appealing to them. They can't imagine doing anything else. Anyone who thinks this is an easy type of business to manage though needs to walk a mile in their shoes for a day.

So You Want To Become A Beef Cattle Farmer

Beef Cattle Farming is a large and important segment of American agriculture and one of the largest industries in the world. Cattle farming enterprises work well with most all other farm production practices such as small grains, fruit orchards, vegetables and others. The livestock will help make efficient use of the many feed   resources that have little alternative use, such as crop residues, marginal cropland,   nvolved s land, rough non-navigable land by wheeled vehicles or rangeland that cannot produce crops other than grass.

If you are lucky enough to own land but work full-time off the farm, a beef cattle farming operation can be the least labor-intensive ways to utilize your land. You will find a cattle or livestock farming   nvolved to be well suited for you to use family or surplus labor. Most all of your labor intensive projects such as , calving, weaning, vaccinations, castration, and weighing may be planned for times when your labor is available. Like when the college kids are home for a school vacation such as July 4th, Thanksgiving or Christmas.

As in most businesses some advance planning may be needed for your farming enterprise to be successful. Some thing to consider are resources like; how much land is available and your level of interest before deciding to engage in the beef cattle business. Accumulate as much information and resources related to your planned business as possible and study everything thoroughly.

Next you will want to try to identify why you want to have a beef cattle farming business. You should then define a mission statement and set some goals to achieve the most constant economic return or personal satisfaction. Do your best to be sure all of this is clearly defined, firmly fixed, is achievable, and can be done within a realistic time frame. Without this your entry into the business may lack meaning that could create a lost objective and cause you to lose focus.

In most cases where you are limited in size and scope due to the number of acres available you may find the most profitable route to be raising registered cattle. Registered cattle of any breed should always command a higher selling price, cost the same amount to feed and do not follow the same ups and downs in the economy that seem to control the commercial cattle operations.

Many newcomers to the beef cattle farming business have found it easier to get established , become a part of the breed community and become recognized as someone who is a serious breeder by starting with a minor breed. You may find those involved within the breed more devoted to their animals than those who raise a breed that everyone seems to have.

Once you are established and become successful you will find there is no better living experience anywhere than being able to live on a few acres where you can have all the comforts of the city plus the enjoyments of the rural life style. And you may be surprised when you discover how much impact a small Beef Cattle Farming business can contribute towards the overall income and reductions in expense.

What Makes a Cattle Breed

To discuss breeds, it is necessary to understand that term. There is no generally accepted definition, scientific or otherwise, of a breed. A 1940 dictionary defines breed as "a race of animals which have some distinctive qualities in common." A 1999 dictionary says "a stock of animals within a species having similar appearance, usually developed by deliberate selection."

There is no "official" recognition of cattle breeds. At one time, the U.S. Department of Agriculture periodically printed a bulletin, "Beef Cattle Breeds." Although inclusion in this publication was often considered official recognition, the 1975 edition of the publication clearly stated, "Inclusion of a breed should not be interpreted as official recognition by the U.S. Department of Agriculture."

There are organizations of breeds, such as the National Pedigreed Livestock Council, but not all breed associations are members. The National Association of Animal Breeders has 108 breed codes for identifying cattle semen. I. L. Mason's World Dictionary of Livestock Breeds lists more than 250 "numerically or historically important" breeds of cattle, along with many less important ones.

One definition of a breed might be animals recorded in an association registry. There are currently some 75 cattle breed registries in the United States. In some cases, there are more than one registry for essentially the same breed.

The only actions needed to start a registry are to adopt specific requirements of eligibility and start recording ancestry. Although those requirements may vary considerably and may not be very stringent, an existing registry may be as good a definition of a breed as any other criteria.

The distinguished animal breeder Dr. Jay Lush, in The Genetics of Populations, said, "A breed is a group of domestic animals, termed such by common consent of the breeders." In short, a "breed" is whatever you say it is.

Miniature cattle breeds are gaining momentum and becoming very popular in the USA. A lot of this popularity can be attributed to the increase in small farms springing up in all areas as more and more people are going for the rural living life style. Minis are better adapted to small holdings, are good converters of grass into beef thus allowing one to grow their own home raised beef without a lot of extra effort.

The development of the breeds takes different routes also. In some breeds you can see the amount of change that can occur as the result of selection for a small number of traits. As an example, Holstein cattle have been selected primarily for milk production and are the highest milk producing cattle in the world. Other breeds have traits that result from natural selection pressure based upon the environment in which they were developed. An example of this might be the N'dama cattle from west Africa. These animals have, through the centuries, developed a resistance to trypanosomiasis or sleeping sickness spread by the tse-tse fly, which is fatal to most other breeds of cattle.

Should we be concerned about preserving information about minor, or relatively unknown, breeds of livestock?

Is there a reason for the preservation of minor breeds of livestock?

Couldn't more improvement be made if there were fewer breeds?

Well, lets go back to our Holstein example again for a moment. While the Holstein clearly has an advantage over other breeds in the production of whole milk, this advantage is based on feeding high levels of cereal grains and pricing that favors low milk-solids content. A drastic change in either of these factors could result in a decrease in the advantage of the Holstein.

Given these conditions perhaps a breed that is currently rare or endangered, such as the Dutch Belted, which displayed excellent milking ability in a grass-based dairy situation in trials in the early 1900's, would find itself on the forefront.

In Australia, composite breeds, such as the Australian Friesian Sahiwal, have been developed which have higher milk production levels than Holsteins in the tropical regions of that country.

Another example might be an increased need for natural resistance to diseases or parasites should a current antibiotic or other treatment become unavailable or ineffective.

An example of this type might be the natural resistance of some breeds of sheep have to internal parasites.

Should anthelmintics become restricted or uneconomical then a breed such as the critically endangered Gulf Coast Native, with the parasite resistance it has developed through natural selection, could be of critical importance in the sheep industry.

In many areas, genetic diversity should be maintained to help meet the potential challenge resulting from changes in production resources and market requirements. We hope that this website will serve as an information resource for the potential of some of these breeds.

A Glimpse into Understanding How Beef Cattle Prices Are Established

Beef Cattle Marketing

A Country Boy's research into Beef Cattle Marketing leads to a better understanding of how Beef Cattle Prices are established. Most of the information is directed towards commercial cattle producers but is equally important for the Seedstock Producer. I believe we can all improve our Beef Cattle Marketing by doing a study of and the understanding of human behavior.

Cattle prices are determined by how much beef people choose to buy and sell in the market place. If people want to buy more beef than is available in the marketing channel, then the price of beef is bid up rationing the beef among buyers. If producers need to sell more beef than people are willing to buy, then the price of beef will be forced downward to move the excess supply.

A lot of cattle producers seem to believe all you have to know or do in the cattle industry to make a profit is to buy low and sell high but believe me the beef industry is more than just the buying and selling cattle. Beef producers add value to their products at each stage in the marketing channel. Cow-calf producers sell a product called a calf. What they are really selling is not the calf but output from the cow and bull and the grass, grain, labor, management and capital used to produce this product called a "calf". Stocker operators buy 300 to 500 pound calves from the cow- calf segment of the industry and put an additional 300 to 400 pounds on them, thus increasing their value to the market place. Feedlots buy the stocker cattle, feed grain to fatten and then sell them at about 1100 to 1300 pounds to the packer. The packer slaughters the animal and breaks the carcass into wholesale cuts for the retailer who in turn sells the beef cuts to the final consumer. Each level within the marketing channel takes the product from the preceding level, modifies it adding value to the product at each subsequent stage.

Marketing is then the cattleman's way of obtaining dollars for the value he adds to the product he produces. After combining the resources he has available to produce the calf, he receives value for the animal by selling it. Failure to successfully market the animal is a waste of his time and the money that he invested in the production phase. Marketing can improve the situation or it can ruin it.

Most producers are good production people, and they dislike the hassle associated with marketing almost as much as keeping records. The fact remains that both record keeping and marketing provide a viable means to increase producer profits. It is often the difficult things in business that make the most money. In beef cattle production, survival depends on a producer being above average in production, marketing, and financial management.

Beef Production And The Marketing System

The U.S. beef production and marketing system consists of production levels and marketing components. Production levels include the cow-calf, stocker, feeder, slaughter-packer, retailer and consumer. This is the physical route the calf takes from the producer to the final consumer. The marketing components include the cash and the futures market. This is the economic route the calf takes from producer through the marketing channel to the retail level for final sale.

Each production level buys or invests in additional

production inputs adding value to the animal. The animal is then sold to the next level in the production system or ownership is retained, where more value is added. This process is repeated until products are finally sold to the consumer at the retail level. It takes time to learn the beef production system and how the product moves through the various levels. Production inputs include physical items like cows, bulls, stockers, feeders, slaughter cattle, carcasses, etc.

It does take a little time to learn the marketing system and how to market beef. Marketing inputs are made up of both information and knowledge. Marketing information to the producer comes in the form of cash prices, futures prices, price outlook, and the supply/demand situation. A producer must know what marketing alternatives are available to him, how to use each alternative, and how to interpret market signals.

The cow-calf producer is the starting point for the beef production and marketing process. The producer invests in land, animals, feed and other inputs to develop his product--the calf. Typically, the cow- calf producer will wean the calf at a weight near 400 pounds or higher. For the spring calving herd, this weaning period is sometime in the fall of the year.

Some cow-calf producers retain ownership of the calves from birth through the stocker phase of the production process and even some maintain ownership through the feedlot. These producers evaluate the profit potential at each production level before deciding to keep their cattle through the next production phase. When their profit objective is reached they sell the cattle. Retained ownership allows the producer the flexibility to reject the market price today in hope of obtaining a better price at a later date. This market alternative can be successful if the cattleman can minimize the costs of growing the animals during the extended ownership period. Also implied in this retained ownership decision is the cattleman's hope that the market does not turn against him.

The vast majority of cow-calf producers normally sell their annual calf crop in the cash market. It has been estimated that a high percentage of the calves sold are through local cash markets. However, cow-calf producers can and do make use of the futures market as an information tool in making marketing decisions without formally entering into a futures contract. The futures market does provide information to the producer about expected market prices and price trends.

Slaughter cow sales volume is greatest during the fall and winter of any year. After calves are weaned cow productivity is generally evaluated. Poor performers are generally culled from the herd to avoid the costs of carrying an open cow through the winter. The availability of pasture and feed sources may create a plus or minus level of activity for this category of cattle.

Stocker Producers

Stocker cattle can be defined as weaned calves that are placed on small grain pastures or placed in feedyards and backgrounded. Beginning stocker cattle weights are normally between 350 and 500 pounds. Finished stocker cattle normally will weigh between 600 and 800 pounds. Stocker operators provide an interim step in the production process--taking these lightweight calves, growing them on cheap feed correcting for any problems that happen at or before weaning.

The stockering phase is not a large part of the cattle

industry in many parts of the country. Inexpensive forages, made available because of rotation requirements with other agronomic crops and by- products from other livestock enterprises, makes stockering attractive when readily available to beef producers. Marketing opportunities available to stocker operations are similar to those at the cow/calf level.

Processor-Packer

Processor-Packers buy finished beef cattle, process them and sell the carcass or boxed beef to retailers. This segment of the beef industry is concentrated in the Midwest among major packing companies, it is estimated that a small group of packers process over 80 percent of the industry's finished beef.

How The Market Determines Cattle Prices

The driving force behind this price discovery process is profit. Every stage of the production marketing channel wants to provide the consumer with a safe, quality product that adds value to the consumer's decision to buy beef. Each segment of the channel adds value to the calf produced to satisfy this consumer need, but each segment also must make a profit.

It is this dichotomy within the industry needing to work together but also each separate segment forced to being profitable that muddies the signals. The poultry industry solved this problem with vertical integration.

Is the market offering a reasonable price? When should cattleman price their cattle? Knowing how prices are determined   may help producers, feeders and packers answer these questions and take advantage of the highest possible price.

Most people get frustrated when economists say that "the forces of supply and demand" determine prices, and as you might   suspect, these economists are only partially correct. If supply and demand were known, prices would be easily determined. The fact is that supply and demand are not known.

In reality, expected supply and demand determines price. Economists refer to beef demand as the amount of beef that will be bought at various prices during a certain time period. As the price of beef increases, the amount bought normally declines. Or, as the price of beef declines, consumers are willing to buy more meat. Thus demand is made up of various components, including quantity and time. Other factors that may affect price are consumer income levels, number of consumers in the market, and prices of related products such as poultry and pork.

Supply also has the two components of quantity and time. Supply is the quantity supplied at various prices during a certain time period. As price increases, producers are willing to produce more and sell more beef. As the price declines, producers are reluctant to sell more beef and over time, will produce less.

So how are prices really determined? Prices are determined by negotiation. These negotiations take place simultaneously at every level of the marketing channel. Consumers have money to spend and they want to purchase beef. But, consumers only have a limited amount of money to spend and they like other goods and services as well as beef. They decide what amount of beef they buy based upon the amount of money they have to spend, the price of beef and their desire to eat beef compared to other food items available to them.

The retailer at any point in time has a certain amount of meat to sell. The retailer puts a price on the meat. The higher the price, the less meat he sells. The lower the price, the more meat he will sell. A price is basically established over time between the consumer and retailer when the amount of meat bought equals the amount the retailer puts in the meat case.

But, the retailers must also anticipate the amount of meat the consumer wants and attempt to purchase that amount from the packer. The packer who has meat in his cooler must sell it. If the packer sells the meat to the retailer, he must also replace it with meat from the feedlot operator in order to keep his cooler full. The packer and the retailer negotiate a price that they are both willing to pay considering the amount of meat available from the feedlot and expected consumer demand anticipated by the retailer.

How do feedlots price feeder cattle? Feedlots price by first estimating demand at the packer level of the marketing channel. Based on the feedlot's view of expected demand for slaughter cattle, the expected supply of slaughter cattle and the resulting packer quoted price, they determine what profit they can make on fat cattle. The expected fat cattle price is then adjusted for anticipated production costs and a profit margin to determine what price the feedlot can offer the stocker operator.

Stocker producers have a limited production period of 120 to about 210 days. Thus, they also have to anticipate the demand for their feeder cattle at the end of this production period. Based on the expected demand for and supply of feeder cattle, the stocker operator estimates a selling price for his cattle. He then must allow for production costs and a profit margin in order to know what to bid for stocker cattle.

The beginning of the production cycle is at the cow-calf level. This is also the ending point of the price discovery process. The cow-calf producer's decision is to take or not to take the offered price. He is frequently referred to as the last rung in the marketing channel or the "price taker". Based on current market prices and future price expectations, the only decisions left to the cow-calf producer are to sell his cattle today or wait until a future date.

Market Information

Successful marketing requires the acquisition of information. Marketing cattle requires the producer to search out information not only about market alternatives and price, but, also estimates of the supply and demand for beef. It is critical that cattlemen obtain an understanding of this market information in order to make useful decisions. Periodically, the USDA releases supply and demand reports for beef, and other livestock and grain commodities that affect beef prices. The most important beef reports are the Cattle on Feed Report and the Cattle Inventory Report.

Cattle On Feed Report

The USDA cattle on feed monthly report estimates the number of cattle and calves on feed for the slaughter market for feedlots with 1,000 one time capacity. Items estimated on the full report include the number of cattle on feed, cattle placed on feed, fed cattle marketed, and other disappearance each month. Cattle on feed are then separated into "kinds" (steer, heifers and cow) on feed and then by sex and weight. The report normally provides cattle on feed numbers for the last three years. It also reports the percentage change in cattle numbers from the previous two years to the present year. First of the month estimates of number of animals on feed are given, then animals placed marketed and other disappearances.

This report provides an estimate of the short run supply and demand picture for beef in the U.S. The difference between the monthly on feed numbers reflects whether or not the supply of finished cattle in feed yards is increasing or decreasing. Over the course of a few months this provides a good estimate of the ability of the economy to absorb beef supplies. Placement numbers also indicate the demand for feeder cattle. Larger placements generally indicate a strong demand for feeder cattle.   Marketing numbers suggest the level of demand for beef by packers and retailers.

Cattle Inventory Report

The USDA cattle inventory report contains USDA's semi-annual estimate of all cattle and calves, cows and heifers that have calved--beef and milk cows, heifers 500 pounds and over--for beef or milk cow replacement and other, steers 500 pounds and over, bulls 500 pounds and over, calves under 500 pounds and the current year calf crop.   The current year's inventory estimated as a percentage of the previous year's estimate is also presented.

USDA's cattle inventory report helps cattlemen determine beef supply trends. The total cattle and heifer retention numbers indicate the potential level of beef in the market channel over the next few years. They indicate cattlemen's expectations about profitability. Increasing heifer retention signals herd expansion due to producer expectations of increasing beef profits. A combination of all of the numbers helps determine where the beef industry is in the cattle cycle.

Market Price Seasonality

Understanding the affect that seasonality has on beef prices also helps the cattle producer develop his marketing plan. Most marketing strategies are dependent upon the producer's calving season. This automatically makes the marketing decision time oriented. Spring calves are sold in the fall and fall calves are sold in the spring. Consequently, the producer's calving practice affects the prices that he is able to achieve each year.

The highest average price typically occurs in late winter and early spring. The lowest average price occurs in the fall. This implies that cow-calf producers that calf in the spring and sell their calves in the fall, sell during the lowest prices of the year. Fall calving operations have the opportunity to sell during the highest seasonal prices, but fall calves face the low gains, extra feed costs and potentially high death loss during the winter months.

The Beef Cycle

The size of the U.S. beef herd does not remain constant over time, rather it increases and decreases depending upon the level of profit achieved by cattle producers. If the industry is profitable cattle producers retain heifers, breed them and in time expand the size of the herd. When the supply of beef exceeds demand, prices fall and the cattle producer diminishes the size of his herd by culling cows and by selling heifers. This process continues through time as the industry tries to adjust the size of the herd to reflect the signals it receives from the forces of supply and demand at work in the market. The term used to explain this process is "the cattle cycle". The cycle is frequently defined as the time between when the cattle numbers are at a lowest point and the next time cattle numbers reach a low point.

The significance of the "cattle cycle" to the beef

industry is that it reflects profit potential to the individual cattle producer. When inventory levels are expanding profits are being made, but at some point in time profit levels will be squeezed out of the market. Prices will fall and adjustments in herd size must be made if the producer is to ready for the next upswing in the "cattle cycle". This is the nature of the beef industry. It will happen again, and producers need to be aware of the cycle and its affect on their profitability.

Cow Slaughter Numbers And Calf Prices

Another relationship may also help us understand why prices react as they do to market forces. This is the relationship between cow slaughter numbers and calf prices. As cow slaughter numbers increase, calf prices decline. Low numbers of slaughter indicate a healthy cow-calf segment within the beef industry. Cattle producers are making a profit; consequently, they will retain cows and heifers in an attempt to build the herd and have more animals to sell.

USDA Hog, Poultry And Crop Reports

Other USDA reports are useful in evaluating intermediate and long-run trends in the beef industry.

Production reports indicate the progress of grain crops, and the supply and demand estimates of these crops, particularly corn and soybeans. Estimates of hog and poultry numbers also provide the cattleman important information of the volume of competing meats today and in the future.

USDA's crop and livestock reports are also readily available to the cattle producers. Cattle and hog slaughter numbers are released each day and are available over the news wires; also, a few local newspapers. Full service commodity brokers provide this information, or if the local sale barn, grain elevator or cotton gin has access to a news wire, the information may be obtained from them.

Feedlot cattle placements and marketings are also available from these market reports. Some farm radio reporters periodically give this information. Also, cattle brokers and merchandisers keep up with how current feedlots are today.

Marketing Alternatives

A cattleman's marketing plan starts with the production of the animal. A solid production program is the basis of the cattle producer's marketing plan. The cattleman must use his knowledge of animal production to produce a product that is acceptable to the market. He must also produce this animal in a timely manner in order to minimize production costs. The cattleman's knowledge, timing and effort are essential in the production of the animal. Knowledge, timing and effort do not guarantee a profit, but they improve the odds. Knowledge, timing and effort are also essential for good marketing.

Marketing, therefore, is a systematic approach toward achieving a reasonable return for the producer's money, labor, management ability and other resources he has invested in the production of his animals. Marketing requires detailed planning and the estimation of costs and prices. Simply put, marketing involves knowing the alternatives, what the alternatives offer, how the alternatives meet the goals of the operation and how best to use each marketing alternative.

The first step in the development of an individual cattle producer's marketing plan is to estimate his cost of producing the calf; it is the MARKET TARGET PRICE. The objective of any plan is to receive a market price that will meet or exceed this cost of production. The producer must keep this market price target in mind when he develops implements and evaluates his marketing efforts.

First and foremost there is not a single magical alternative that cures all of the producer's marketing problems. There are alternatives that if used wisely under reasonable conditions have served producers well for many years. The question is which of the available alternatives fits your needs. The Alternatives available include: cash sales, futures contracts, option contracts, retained ownership or a combination of these.

What marketing alternatives are available to the cattle producer depends upon the stage of production. Some alternatives are used more often at one production level than another. There are profitable alternatives available at every production level. The cattleman's job is to find each alternative and evaluate its ability to make his operation a profit

Producer Marketing Alternatives
Producers may choose to market their weanling calves through a local or regional sale, sell to an off the farm

buyer, or forward contract with a buyer for future delivery. It is also possible to use the futures markets to market weanling or stocker calves.

The objective is to market grass pasture, labor, capital and management by selling calves, cull cows and cull bulls. Generally the majority of producers attempt to satisfy this objective through their local auction barn. They do so for various reasons including closeness to the farm, small number of animals to market, time it takes to evaluate other markets and the fact that the local auction is a form of entertainment.

The local auction is also the most cussed form of marketing in the cattle industry. Many producers' say that they have taken their animal to the local auction barn only to get ripped off. The fact is that the producer frequently does not know the market and is not willing to put forth the effort to gain an understanding of the market. With a little knowledge the producer would start to see what he can do to improve his situation. By evaluating market alternatives, including the profitable use of a local auction, he can improve the profit from his beef operation.

Another cash market option available to producers is retained ownership. It can be used for his annual calf crop or stocker operation. It can also be used for the "best" of his heifer and bull calves destined for sale to other producers as replacement animals. The market price target is useful in evaluating whether or not the producer should participate in retained ownership.

Retained ownership decisions compare the sale of the calf today with a future sale at a heavier weight. Several factors come into play in this decision. The producer must know the prices for the light weight calf and the expected price for the heavier calf. In addition he must know the cost of producing the weanling calf and the cost of carrying it the additional days.

A good producer marketing strategy is to establish a reputation for producing above average stockers or breeding stock. Development of a sound production program requires a long-term commitment on the part of the producer. Good breeding stock or the development of a quality stocker program doesn't occur overnight. A good producer should take advantage of his "good name". Surveys of cattle buyers indicate that an important criterion in price determination is the producer's reputation. A good reputation normally brings buyers to the farm eliminating the need to sell at auction.

Having buyers come to the farm to purchase cattle provides a marketing opportunity for both buyer and seller. The seller can reduce shrink and avoid commission costs. The buyer obtains an animal that has a known parentage and production philosophy, and minimal stress. On farm sales are a good opportunity for cow-calf producers to market their animals and build a reputation with buyers.

The producer can also use the futures market to lock in a price or shift the chance of an adverse price change. However, futures contracts are not readily adapted to lightweight calves. The difference between the futures price and the local price for these lightweight calves can be quite large. This wide difference makes it difficult to accurately fix a price.

Choosing the right market to meet your objective can be difficult. This is where the development of a market target price becomes important. The producer has some bench mark to evaluate local market prices against what it costs him to produce the calf. Two things have been accomplished: first, the producer is capable of evaluating the price the local market is paying for calves similar to his and, secondly he is able to really understand if this marketing alternative can successfully play a role in his overall beef objectives.

Putting It All Together

We have considered many factors that are integral components in developing a successful marketing plan for cattle producers. It is now time to put these factors into a plan of action and show how a marketing plan is actually developed. The marketing plan does not need to be real fancy or complex but, it does need to be well thought out and adapted to meet the needs of your cattle operation. Clearly, the plan should suggest what you want out of your involvement in the cattle business and how you intend to get there. There are many ways to classify a market plan. Here is one plan with only six simple steps:

Know what you have to market
Develop your cost of production and market target price
Analyze the market environment
Review available market alternatives

Compare market alternatives against your operation's goals

Make your decision and market your cattle

Know What You Have To Market

In order to understand where you want to go in your business you must first determine where you are today. Inventory your herd. Decide what classes of cattle, i.e., steers, heifers, bulls, cows, etc., you are going to sell this year. Next determine the sale time. Compare sale opportunities with feed needs and production costs as well as expected prices.

Inventorying your herd will force you to look at your cattle in some detail. There are several characteristics you will need to consider when you review your cattle herd. This process allows you to consider how your herd compares with the average cattle sold in your area. Separate and count your cattle. Determine the number of good ones and "bottom enders". The buyers are doing this whether you sell on farm or go through the local auction. Once you have made this inventory list you are ready to compare your animals with the market. You now know the number of head by color, sex, weight, frame size and their faults. Most producers say they don't know the how and why behind the price they get for their cattle. It is easy. They are right in front of you all you have to do is classify and know what characteristics receive premiums and which ones are discounted.

Some of characteristics to look for and an estimate of price discounts per cwt:

Muddy Hair Coat, $1.00 to 2.00
Lameness, $10.00 to 15.00
Stale Cattle, $4.00 to 6.00
Sick Cattle, $10.00 to 20.00
Bad Eyes, $5.00 to 8.00
Horns, $1.00 to 5.00
Bulls, $3.00 to 10.00
Overly Fleshy Cattle, $1.00 to 3.00
Excessive Fill, $2.00 to 4.00
Breed Composition, $1.00 to 10.00
Frame Size
Small, $5.00 to 10.00
Lower Third of Medium, $1.00 to 2.50
Upper Third of Large, $1.00 to 2.50

Always keep in mind that price discounts can be quite

variable from market to market. They frequently depend upon market location and prevailing market conditions. Generally speaking, cattle are discounted for poor nutrition, sickness, horns, sex and lameness. Breed composition also leads to discounts in some markets. Straight bred cattle of all breeds are discounted as compared to good crossbreds. High percentage ear breeds are discounted as much as $5.00 to $10.00 per cwt and in some markets spotted or light color cattle are also discounted.

Some characteristics are always discounted: sick cattle, horns, bulls, etc. These discounts are the market's way of signaling the need for change. Producers need to realize that discounting implies that the market considers a particular trait unacceptable today. The market's feeling about this trait may also change over time. A once discounted trait may become acceptable at some point in time. Conversely, a trait once considered acceptable may receive a discount in the future. The market uses this discounting procedure to reflect it's feelings about the cattle being produced and their value to the industry today.

The inventorying effort can point out to the producer the best and the worst in his cattle. It might even keep him from continually fooling himself. Producers seldom talk about what they were paid for their bottom end cattle; instead they like to talk about the one that brought the highest sale price. Unfortunately, not all of their cattle brought this high price, but it took the same dollars to raise the bottom calf as it did the top one.

Develop Your Cost Of Production And Market Target Price

We have talked at length about estimating your cost of production and developing a market target price. It can not be emphasized enough that after knowing what you have to sell, knowing the amount of dollars that you have in the calf is the next step in any marketing effort. You can't make an informed decision without knowing the cost of producing the calf.

Analyze The Market Environment

Analyzing the market environment is a fancy way of saying that you need to understand the forces of supply and demand and how they influence cattle prices. You must be aware of how the cattle cycle, cattle inventory numbers, hog and poultry numbers and the price of corn influences cattle prices. In short, this is knowledge of the market forces that you are facing at the time of sale. It changes each year. Cattle producers must become involved in the market and develop an expectation of price levels.

Don't be like the producer who asks what is going on in the cattle market because he had taken some calves to the sale barn this year and received $30 per cwt lower than last year. He had no advance understanding or expectations because he had not done any homework. He could have asked about prices from a neighbor or even looked in the newspaper. His last exposure to the cattle market was the year before when he took his calves to market.

Review Available Market Alternatives

Many factors influence whether or not a market is acceptable. As you evaluate market alternatives ask yourself some of the following questions. What type of cattle will this specific market take? You need to sell a certain number of animals of a particular weight, color, frame size, sex, and health and management status. Will your cattle sell well at this market or are they going to be discounted because of one or more reasons. Do you have the ability to influence the way your animals are presented to the buyer? Auctions generally sell single lots--can you group your calves? On farm sales and some regional sales automatically grade, sort and group calves by sex, weight and color. Do you have enough cattle to sort by class?

What about the buyers? Who are their customers? Are they buying for only a few customers, i.e., a packer, or are they servicing a broad customer base that can take wide range of weights, ages, and frame sizes? Take the time to meet and talk with these buyers. Find out what they normally buy and what they want to see in a calf. Match his needs against your cattle inventory.

Remember you also sell cull cows and bulls. This market is quite different than your calf market. Buyers are different and the main price determining factors are health and weight. Cow grades are based primarily on carcass yield potential. Bigger carcasses that yield a high amount of meat are paid a premium over smaller carcasses.

There are also other considerations you need to evaluate. These factors may not directly affect the price you receive for your cattle but they can indirectly influence the number of dollars that you finally put into your pocket. What about the handling facilities? Will they let you work your cattle in an easy manner or will your cattle be stressed in the unloading or loading process? Stressed cattle can show signs of sickness and frequently lose weight. Can you feed and water your cattle if they are penned for any length of time prior to their sale? What about the records that are kept on your cattle as they go through the sale? Are they accurate? How soon after the sale are you paid? And how is the amount of shrink determined?

Review your marketing alternatives. Take some time to see if there are other market outlets that you can use. If there are, evaluate them critically, not just if they can provide you with a better price than your current market. The time to review these options is not the day before you plan to take your calves to the sale but, sometime earlier so you can have time to thoroughly review and understand these options.

Compare Market Alternatives Against Your Operation's Goals

Once you have analyzed the marketing alternatives available to you, compare their potential to your stated business objectives. Will they fit your operation? Are they physically possible or do you have to significantly change the way you do business to utilize an alternative?

Make Your Decision And Market Your Cattle

Finally, make a decision and market your calves. Don't try to second guess your decision. If you do well keep you will want to keep this alternative for next year. If it did not pan out then scratch this alternative and go on. You learn from your mistakes and every year is different in the cattle business. Marketing is a planned event that is reviewed every year, changed if necessary, but constantly improved.

Last, but not least, what about retained ownership? It is a marketing alternative. Would it be profitable for you to keep these calves until next spring? They will weigh more. The information required to analyze a retained ownership decision is the same as that used to evaluate any other market. First, estimate the cost of gain. Then compare what you can get for the calves today against a spring sale. The futures market and knowledge of the basis will help develop a spring price estimate.

Summary

Most producers are good production people and they dislike the hassle associated with marketing. But, in beef cattle production survival depends on a producer being above average in production, marketing and financial management.

A successful beef marketing effort includes at least six steps: knowing what you have to market, knowing the costs of production, knowing the market environment, reviewing alternative marketing actions, comparing alternatives against management goals, and making a decision and staying with the decision.

These steps allow a cattle producer to inventory his herd and review its strengths and weaknesses. Reviewing the market environment also provides information about the basic supply and demand factors that influence prices. Comparison of market alternatives allow the opportunity to match the operation's strengths against what the market is offering this year. Finally, a marketing decision must be made. This step wise procedure will allow any cattleman to make a better and more informed decision when marketing his cattle.

Beef Cattle Marketing For Ranchers

Marketing beef cattle is a make or break enterprise for many ranchers and farmers. Management decisions need to be made on an almost daily basis. Proper marketing requires knowing the latest prices and being able to interpret current trends.

For a profitable operation in the beef cattle industry, the following are a few of the considerations that must be carefully thought out and planned.

• Deciding if the present prices justify changing cattle production
  • How to get the most money for the stock being sold
  • How to pay the lowest cost for additional cattle
  • How to operate the cattle production in the most cost efficient manner
  • Choosing when, where and how to market current stock
  • Calculating profit margins
  • Weighing both long term and short-term production needs
  • Choosing the types of beef cattle to produce

Beef Prices

Cattle prices depend largely upon the performance of the beef and slaughter market. One of the top factors that impacts the prices paid for cattle is the present demand and supply levels. The retail area is where the negotiations for beef cattle prices constantly fluctuate. There are several large beef sellers who are consistently involved in this mix. These organizations include giants like IBP, ConAgra, and Smithfield. They are creating prices based on their own negotiations with big retail outlets like Publix, WalMart, Meijer's, and Food Lion.

While the suppliers of fresh beef understand the prices and costs of supplies, feed and quality meat it is the retailers who understand the price consumers will pay. It appears that new negotiations can occur at any time but most of these discussions and pricing agreements take place weekly. It is important that everyone understand that the decisions made by the major packers and distributors and the largest retailers is the beginning point for the remainder of people involved in the beef industry. The price point that is established between retailer and packer will then be used to establish prices for all remaining players. This is known as "the trickle down effect".

The Packer/ Producer Level

Beef cattle prices at the market level may be set a few weeks ahead of time. This means that all of the packers should be aware of what prices the different cuts of beef will actually bring. The "Cut out Value" is the price that will be brought by all of the different beef cuts. A shift in market price of only a nickel a pound can mean $40 dollars more a head for producers of cattle with 800-pound carcasses. Producers who are in the loop and keeping up to date on the latest price can be paid the extra money if the market is not flooded with extra beef products already. Savvy cattlemen who know how much money the packers are being paid can determine if the market prices will support their own higher price demands. They can negotiate with the packers of their choice if they are not locked into iron-clad contracts with one particular company.

Meat Packers Pay -2 different Ways

There are 2 different methods used by packers who are purchasing marketed beef cattle. The first is the live-weight, cash transaction and the second method is called grid pricing.

• Live-weight pricing is when the packer buyers check out a group of cattle brought in as a single lot. They will estimate the value and quality and then they will present the producer with a price offer for the whole lot. If a cattleman places a group of cattle in one of the pens and the buyer figures that 90% of the lot will be Certified as Angus Beef, he will calculate a price for all of the group. Let's say that the going price for USDA Choice Cattle is presently $70 per each hundred pounds of weight. This means that Angus Beef Grade might fetch an additional $3 per hundredweight for $73. An adjustment will have to be made for those animals that will not make the grade as Angus Beef. The packers may average the price for all of the animals to $72, which would make a 1000 pound steer worth $720. If there are 10 animals in the group and the total weight is 10000 pounds the cash price paid to the producer would be $7200. This means that more money will be paid out for per head to compensate for the increased quality of the higher graded cattle.

• The grid pricing method is becoming more common and this is money paid per carcass pound. All of the animals are graded and the prices are calculated based on quality, the grading yield, the weight of the carcasses and whether or not any Angus grades or dark cutters are in the lot group. Because there are so many individual factors taken into consideration with grid pricing the per head price can vary by as much as $200.

Beef Cattle Marketing - More On Marketing Your Cattle

It may not be easy to determine how and where to market your animals. The choice of market outlet depends on the class and grade of the cattle. Thus, the method of marketing usually is different for fed cattle, feeder, or purebred cattle.

There are many different methods of marketing cattle, but most livestock in the United States are marketed through one of three channels: direct, auction, or carcass grade and weight basis. The direct and auction markets are for both fed and feeder cattle, while the carcass grade and weight basis is primarily for fed cattle. Purebred cattle usually are sold at special breed auctions or private sales.

If you have a feeder or stocker enterprise your product is one or more 700 to 900 pound calves. You may choose to keep the animals and feed them as a market cattle enterprise or if you do not have the desire or resources to do so; you will need to market them. If you only have a few cattle of this type your marketing options are limited. To ensure cattle are marketed optimally discuss your options with those experienced in the business and keep up to date on market reports via newspaper or radio. You can sell them at a local auction or sell them by private treaty by advertising them in the paper, word of mouth or an advertisement on bulletin boards at the local feed store or wherever cattlemen gather.

Auction

Livestock auctions or sales barns are trading centers where animals are sold by public bidding to the buyer who offers the highest price per hundredweight or per head. Auctions may be owned by individuals, partnerships, corporations, or cooperative associations.

Direct marketing (country dealers)

Direct selling, or country selling, refers to sales of livestock directly to packers, local dealers, or farmers without the use of agents or brokers. The sale usually takes place on the farm, ranch, feedlot, or some other non-market buying station or collection yard.

You may choose to have your cattle finished and butchered for home consumption. You can also have them slaughtered by a custom packer and sell them to individuals cut and wrapped which is not always economical. Extension personnel can assist you in determining the economics of home raised beef.

This method does not involve a recognized market. Sellers who direct-market should be aware of possible regulations regarding the private sale of breeding animals or beef for consumption.

Niche marketing

A producer often can develop a local or regional market for certain cuts of beef or specialty beef products. If this interests you, check into meat handling requirements, inspections, and permits that may be necessary. This type of marketing usually takes time to develop and also may require a consistent seasonal or yearly supply.

Grades of carcass beef

Carcass beef sold to wholesale and retail outlets usually is graded to determine the quality and price. There are two categories of grades for beef: yield grade and quality grade.

Yield grade

Yield grade, or cutability designates the yield of

trimmed retail cuts from the carcass. Factors determining yield grade are:

- Fat thickness over rib eye
- Rib eye area
- Kidney, pelvic, and heart fat (KPH), calculated as a percentage
- Hot carcass weight

Yield grades range from 1 to 5, with 1 being the leanest and 5 the fattest (requiring the most trimming).

Quality grade

Quality grades designate various characteristics of meat and give the buyer a guide to tenderness, juiciness, and flavor. Grades separate beef into groups that are somewhat uniform in quality and composition.

The quality grade of a beef carcass is determined by physiological maturity and marbling. The age of the animal affects the tenderness of the meat.

Quality assurance

When consumers go to the store to purchase beef, they want quality meat, free of bruises, dark spots, abscesses, or lesions. Quality assurance means that beef producers pay attention to the factors that contribute to quality meat, produce a beef product that is free from defects, and ensure that consumers get the quality they want.

When you raise beef cattle to sell to a feedlot or packer, you are selling a food product. The handling, management, and environment on your farm or ranch affect the quality of the product and what the consumer ultimately buys in the store. Poorly designed facilities and equipment can increase the number of cuts, puncture wounds, and bruises on beef animals. Corrals or chutes with sharp corners or protruding nails or bolts should be altered or repaired.

You must keep records to document that vaccines and antibiotics were administered properly. Pay attention to withdrawal times on labels as well as dosage. Use only vaccines and drugs approved by the U.S. Food and Drug Administration and the state Department of Agriculture. Your veterinarian or Extension agent can advise you of proper injection sites and procedures to reduce abscesses and lesions.

Raising Beef Cattle for Profit - Some Ideas To Challenge Your Thinking

You will find raising beef cattle for profit to be a little more challenging these days and getting more so every passing day. Cattle farmers and ranchers in today's modern high tech environment need to teach themselves to think outside the norm. That is where to find the more profitable niches related to raising cattle for profit.

One of the most important and probably the most difficult things to get yourself started with is to write yourself a business plan that predicts an end result that is profitable. Doing the research and getting it down on paper will almost always result with a profitable plan.

Discovering your very own niche to set you apart from other cattle producers is one thing to think about. An example niche might be "All Natural", "Grass Fed", "Home Grown", and "All Organic".

In some cases it may be prudent to setup a separate entity when it is felt there may be a need to minimize liability. Protect your other assets.

We will focus this article on one of the highest income producing methods which is direct sales of your finished product, beef directly to the consumer. This is true because you own the cattle from beginning to end. marketing your beef can increase your income because it not only adds a new enterprise to your ranch, but helps you retain ownership through all phases of production.

For direct marketing you will need to locate a processing plant as close to your marketing area as possible. It is much more economical to transport a live animal a few miles than packaged product. Inquire about and learn as much as possible about the plant's capabilities to process, package and make the beef available for customer pickup. A good choice is usually a smaller plant that provides a USDA inspected product. As you begin to grow there may be a need to occasionally consult with a meat scientists to help ensure consistency.

Create a good image within your community and the industry as a whole. Do this by being sure to keep your cattle farm clean and presenting a pleasant experience for all visitors. Keep all feeding facilities and other equipment in good repair at all times (ready for prospective customer showing at a moments notice). Prospective customers may want to view your actual feeding operations.

Other positive image ideas would be a powerful logo for your business. Think in terms of a logo or product label that might lend itself to other advertising items like Bumper Stickers, T Shirts, Caps, Coffee Mugs and more.

When direct marketing to the end consumer you should search for an area with little or no competition if at all possible. Having your own unique area for your product or business always helps.

Because more beef is purchased by women than men it would help to teach yourself some of the finer points in marketing to them. Study and learn as many ways as you can to get into the mindset of "Buying Food For The Family," after all, this is where your product ends up.

Do your research and determine as close as possible to who your customers will be. Then taylor your approach to their needs and wants. Try to learn their cultures and life styles and then you will be able to market directly to those.

If you elect to sell by package or in small lots you may want to determine your market for the lesser cuts of meat and do most of your advertising towards moving those. The more prime or in demand cuts will usually take care of their own market.

It is always a good idea to start on a small scale and plan a slow steady growth pattern. Expect profits to be small at the start. This will also be to your advantage as it will allow you to make adjustments as you grow in size and experience and learn your specific marketing situation.

And last but not least be sure to include all of the above into your research to develop a business plan.

Developing a Registered Cattle Herd

If your objective is to raise registered cattle and supply breeding animals to other cattle producers, it may be necessary to make large capital investments in purebred stock. Development of a registered herd means that both the sire and dam must be purebred and registered with the same national breed association. You must keep accurate records and register the desirable purebred calves to be retained for breeding stock.

If you raise bulls for the beef industry, you must develop a selection program based on characteristics of economic importance, such as fertility, mothering ability, ease of calving, growth rate, and carcass merit. Also, use great care in the selection of breeding females, as considerable time and expense are involved.

Competition is keen with already-established herds. However, there are successful registered herds with only 30 to 50 cattle. As in most all enterprises this one is no exception and the breeder who pays closest attention to details and customer needs will always be the most successful.

Sale of breeding stock is the main source of income from registered cattle. Care and management of registered cattle is more intensive than for commercial cattle. Establishing a breeding herd is a long-range program. It also requires more land than a simple steer or heifer feeding program. Consider how your available resources match your long-term objectives. There must be adequate feed, water, and fences to accommodate a year-round operation.

Purchasing cattle

There are many sources of good cattle, both registered and commercial. Usually it's best to purchase from a successful and reputable breeder. They usually sell only sound cattle as breeding animals and they are helpful in giving advice to less experienced producers.

If you are inexperienced, it might be best to buy good, young, bred cows that have calved at least once. This reduces problems associated with calving heifers. If you purchase open heifers, you should breed them to a bull that has the genetics for easy calving.

The major concern of cattle producers is profit. Because your entire program depends on the fitness of the breeding animals, it is essential to maintain good herd health by not allowing the cattle to become too fat or too thin. Cows do not milk as well and may have problems calving or getting bred if they are overweight or underweight. Bulls that are not in good condition may perform poorly during the breeding season.

Developing a Commercial Cattle Herd

The criteria for selection, or selling points, of good cows for your commercial cattle herd depend on size, quality, age, condition, stage of pregnancy, and market price. You should select breed and cow size to match your feed resources and topography. Local ranchers or Extension personnel can give you an idea of what breeds are best suited to your area.

Crossbreeding (mating animals from two or more breeds) can be an advantage in a commercial cow herd. Capitalizing on the merits of several breeds, plus the extra vigor from crossbred calves, may give you a competitive edge in the market. Remember that advances in genetic merit probably will not be realized for several years.

Purchasing cattle

There are many sources of good cattle, both registered and commercial. Usually it's best to purchase from a successful and reputable breeder. They usually sell only sound cattle as breeding animals and they are helpful in giving advice to less experienced producers.

If you are inexperienced, it might be best to buy good, young, bred cows that have calved at least once. This reduces problems associated with calving heifers. If you purchase open heifers, you should breed them to a bull that has the genetics for easy calving.

Managing a cow-calf herd

It is ideal to have a controlled breeding season, rather than allowing the bull to run with the cows continuously. A 45- to 60-day breeding season is recommended. The resulting shortened calving season increases the possibility of having a uniform set of calves to sell at market time. Cattle of similar breeding and size usually bring more money. Another advantage is that you can concentrate your work with cows during calving into a short span, instead of having it strung out for months.

Cattle have a 283-day gestation period. Select breeding dates so that cows will calve at the time of year you desire. Considerations in determining calving season include weather conditions and the ability to match feed resources with the cows' requirements. In most areas late fall or winter calving usually is not desirable because rain causes wet, muddy lots and pastures. The adverse weather may increase the incidence of calf scours and pneumonia. Late summer calving is a common practice because of the ideal weather. However, you must feed a high quality ration to nursing cows and calves during winter, when only harvested feeds are available. This greatly increases feed costs. Calving in the spring allows the cows to utilize rapidly growing range and pasture, thus eliminating harvesting costs. However, spring calves may be too young to use all of the milk the cow provides as a result of the excellent nutrition she is receiving. Your Extension agent can discuss the pros and cons of calving seasons with you.

Commercial Cattle Herd Sire

A quality sire is essential to maintain a good, healthy herd. The rule of thumb is 1 bull to 25 cows. The ratio varies depending on the bull's age and health, and the size of pasture.

Small herd owners have the following options for obtaining a good-quality bull:

* You can buy a bull in cooperation with another ranch.
* You can lease or borrow a sire from a neighbor.

However, using a bull increases the risk of diseases. Bulls also may pose a safety risk, so treat them with respect.

Another good breeding option is artificial insemination (AI). If you use this method, you should synchronize estrus in the herd for a shortened calving season. This process may require the aid of a veterinarian.

The last consideration of the breeding season is pregnancy testing the cows. The test helps determine which cows should be culled from the herd to avoid the costs of wintering a cow that is not pregnant. Veterinarians offer pregnancy testing services.

Calving

This aspect of beef cattle management requires experience and skill. If you are inexperienced, it is recommended that you contact your veterinarian and/or Extension agent for advice on calving management. Most Extension agents can provide you with a printed Cow Calf Management Guide.

Working the calves

One of the simplest ways to add to the value of your calves is to make sure they are well fed, properly castrated, dehorned, vaccinated, and clearly identified. The most important thing to remember when working calves is to stress them as little as possible. You can learn how to castrate, dehorn, and give vaccinations under the supervision of an experienced cattle producer or veterinarian.

A good vaccination program also is vital to herd health and performance. Your Extension agent and veterinarian are good sources of information on this subject.

Weaning

Weaning is accomplished by separating calves from their mothers. Calves should be weaned at approximately 7 to 8 months of age. This gives the cow time to regain body condition after nursing.

Calves need an ample supply of fresh water and feed. Some producers prefer to creep feed calves prior to weaning. This may help encourage the calves to begin feeding on their own after weaning.

Keeping performance records

Keeping records enables you to cull poor performers and maintain good overall herd health and vigor. Examples of helpful calf records include birth weight, weaning weight, and average daily gain. Your Extension agent is a good resource for help.

Combinations of breeding, growing, and feeding

Most calves produced in small commercial herds are marketed as weaned calves weighing from 450 to 600 pounds. Other options include the following:

• Wean the calves, winter them, and sell them as yearlings.

• Creep feed calves while the animals are still nursing, put them on full feed after weaning, and then sell them as slaughter cattle at 12 to 16 months of age.

• Wean calves, winter them on a growing ration, then graze them during spring and early summer and finish them to slaughter weight at 18 to 24 months of age.

Grassfed Cattle

Livestock producers have been keeping track of consumer trends and many of them have become vocal advocates about raising grass fed beef cattle. Letting these docile animals graze in fresh, green pasturelands is a healthy and productive method of working in harmony with nature. Fresh forage and sweet, green grasses are the ideal food sources for beef cattle.

Cattle that have been fed in this manner are less likely to become ill or contract a disease and their weight gain is compatible with those that are fed grains and other supplements. Letting a herd of cattle graze and forage for tasty greens in the open pastures is a sure way to produce healthy and heavily muscled animals.

With more and more of the health conscious public veering away from artificial additives and chemicals, the market has become a hot spot for ranchers and owners who have been raising grass fed beef cattle to sell. Many of the top livestock producers are eager to show that they have been listening to the concerns of the public. They can document that their animals have been given only natural grasses to eat and no grains or other supplements.

Due to the careful maintenance and management of these herds, the cows and steers have matured into healthy, prime livestock that will fetch top dollar at market. Buyers can purchase these naturally fed animals and they will be able to let the consumers know that this quality meat is far superior in taste and texture.

In order to be sold with a description like "grass fed cattle", any livestock must have an owner or agent present who will be willing to sign an affidavit attesting to this fact. This is to document with a sworn statement that the "grass fed cattle" have not been given any enhancers, steroids, grains or other unallowable products.

If a rancher has been raising grass fed beef cattle and gives the animals an antibiotic or food supplement at any time then they have forfeited the right to include the words "grass fed" in the livestock description. There are some substantial penalties that can be meted out if anyone attempts to fraudulently sell grain fed beef for the higher paying "grass fed" prices.

These well cared for, properly nourished cattle can command some top dollars on the open market. Grain fed livestock saves a good deal of money in food costs during the 1-2 years it takes for them to reach maturity. There are a few owners who try to demand even higher prices than the set rate but the beef market is stable and current prices have little variation on the day. These cows and steers will have mature weights of 800-1300 pounds. Although they eat only forage material, a 1200-pound cow will graze through about 5 tons of greens in just one year. Considering the amount of grass eaten, an 800-pound cow could be considered very weight conscious.

When consumers buy grass fed beef, they expect a lean and healthy protein source. Most of the meat is very lean with rich flavor and good taste. There are a few cattle breeds that can still put some fat on their frames even on this restricted diet. The fat that occurs on cows raised on grasses is healthier than the fat marbling that is usually present in grain fed cattle.

Feeder Stocker Enterprise

A feeder stocker or backgrounding operation pastures or feeds calves until they reach 750 to 800 pounds. Then they are sold to a feedlot for finishing.

Purchasing feeder stocker calves in spring and selling them in the fall as feeder cattle may be a way to convert pasture to profit for those with a surplus of grass but not a lot of facilities. But managing pasture, animals, costs, and markets plays a key role in determining the level of profit producers can expect.

The enterprise budget must take into consideration costs of labor, pasture, minerals, implants, marketing, veterinary, pumping water, interest, and miscellaneous needs. Farmers or producers who wish to wish to evaluate a stocker enterprise's profitability need to know how much they can pay for calves in the spring and still make a profit in the fall. For example, a producer who is buying beef stockers with expectations of selling them in the fall for $0.65 per pound with a daily rate of gain of 2.2 pounds per day can pay up to $0.93 per pound for calves and usually break even.

financial success of a stocker operation will depend . some factors which are largely outside of the producer's control, like weather and price spread. Some producers use hedging instruments in the form of forward, futures, or options contracts to protect their prices. Others follow market reports closely or rely on many years of marketing knowledge to decide how and when to sell their cattle to receive the best prices. But by having some control over costs, rates of gain, and type of stockers, producers can estimate their profits based on spring calf prices and fall feeder prices.

Some excellent enterprises are solely pasture operations. Weaned calves or yearlings are purchased in early spring, go on pasture when the grass is ready, and are sold when the pasture season is over. On the other hand, calves cost less in the fall; therefore, depending on the cost of winter feed, fall may be the best time to purchase cattle for the next pasture season.

In these calf and yearling enterprises, purchase price and selling price greatly influence profitability. It is recommended that you ask an experienced cattle buyer to assist in purchasing animals that best suit your type operation, land, and resources.

Managing newly purchased calves

When you purchase calves for a growing or feeding operation, keep them in an area that allows you to observe them for 2 weeks. This enables you to prevent the spread of disease.

Calves should have access to plenty of water and feed. Working the calves requires a lot of patience, as they are easily excited and stressed. Your veterinarian or Extension agent can help you develop a health program that lowers the risk of disease for newly received calves.

of

Market Beef Enterprise - Selling Finished Product Direct To Consumer

In a steer or heifer market beef operation, you purchase 500 to 600 pound feeder calves after weaning at approximately 7 to 10 months of age. They can then be fed out and marketed in less than a year from the time of purchase. Thus, the investment on each calf is returned within a comparatively short time. This type of operation may not require much land, but adequate facilities are essential so that animals can be kept comfortable and under control.

Direct marketing is selling food and farm products directly to consumers without using an intermediary. This may include direct sales to grocery stores, restaurants, door-to-door and freezer sales and Internet marketing.

According to USDA's Economic Research Service, general livestock farms sold less than 1 percent of total livestock sales by means of direct marketing in 1992. More current information will be available when the 2002 Farm Census is analyzed. More than $3 million in sales was

sales. Direct marketing of livestock
ᵣnmon as other vegetables and melons,
ᵣause livestock require further processing.
ᵣge of farms with direct sales is higher in more
ᵣ counties.

However, direct marketing can provide prices for producers higher than typical wholesale prices, yet below supermarket prices. Interest in food safety, the environment, people wishing to purchase local products and alternative agriculture has also supported this growth. Consumers enjoy dealing face-to-face with the producers of the products they are purchasing. This trend relates to traceability and accountability. The ability to trace a product to the original source is a critical food safety issue and provides consumers assurance that their food is safe and wholesome because they know the individual who produced it for them.

Increasing numbers of producers and producer groups are reaching new consumers using the Internet. With widespread sales of home computers, an estimated 60 percent of the U.S. population has Internet access. More consumers are shopping over the Internet. According to the

U.S. Census Bureau, total e-commerce sales during 2
were estimated at $32.6 billion.

Beef that is sold over the Internet must be processed in
federally inspected plants. If the meat is processed in a state
inspected facility, it is only legal to sell meat within that
state.

Farmers' markets continue to grow in the United States.
According to the USDA, there were more than 3,100
farmers' markets in 2002, an increase of 79 percent from
1994. Farmers' markets are beneficial to farm operations
that have less than $250,000 in annual receipts.

Direct marketed beef will be affected by the growing
trend of more meals consumed outside of the home.
Expenditures on away-from-home food now account for
about 47 percent of total U.S. food expenditures. The
National Restaurant Association projects away-from-home
food expenditures will exceed at-home food expenditures
by 2010. Possible implications and opportunities could be
further explored. Perhaps producer groups will want to
consider providing pre-cooked, easy to reheat meat
products, or develop other products that can meet the needs

Bottle Calf Enterprise

Contrary to what you may have thought, you don't nee a great deal of money or pasture to get started raising cattle. Not if you do it the bottle calf way. However, you may want to start with only two or three until you get the hang of it. Then why not consider a small start with a bottle calf or two. You will learn a great deal through trial and error at first. But in the end you may remain convinced that the "bottle calf method" is by far the easiest, most economical and most educational way to get started in small scale cattle farming.

Whenever possible you should buy a bottle calf directly from the original owner. You will also want to keep close contact with local dairies because some may sell part of calves at birth. Buying a bottle calf direct from a dairy is usually an advantage because most times the calf has been allowed to nurse for a few days, in which case it received a good dose of colostrum or first milk that it needs for a good start in life.

You can sometimes also purchase calves at feedlots, because some cows that are brought to the lots for fattening

` managers don't want to bother with

 to keep in mind about large feedlots

 calf born in one of these huge "meat

 get very little care and not even a first

 ou ask the manager or someone at his direction

ify you immediately when a calf is born.

Another source for baby calves is your local livestock auction but some feel you should buy here only only if you have time, money and extra pens to gamble with. You never really know what you're getting when you buy an animal at the regular local auction. When buying at this type of sale you should try to arrive several hours before the bidding starts and don't buy any calf that you haven't checked close up first.

What should you look for in a newborn bottle calf prospect as you carefully check it over? Stand it up and run your hands over its entire body to check for swellings, enlarged bones, or deformities. Put an ear to the calf's rib cage to try to detect any respiratory problems. Check it's navel for signs of infection. As a final check, you may want to stand back and give the calf a once over to see if it's eyes are bright and clear with no clouds or white spots. Are it's ears up and alert, not drooped, its nose should be free of any discharge. Usually a healthy calf will also suck your finger, give it a the finger test. Is it lively? A sick or poor quality calf will usually appear overly docile.

If weather warrants you should keep the new calf warm and dry. Don't expect an already stressed calf to ride several miles in the back of a pickup in cold or rainy weather and be in good health with the needed survival instincts. Some provision must be made for keeping the calf dry and warm from the time you buy it until you can get it home to a comfortable new draft-free pen.

Upon arrival at the farm it is a good idea to immediately isolate the new calf from the rest of your herd. You may find it to be easier than you think to wipe out a large portion of an existing herd by bringing in a strange calf that harbors disease or germs.

For early shelter a simple three sided lean to type will do to keep the new bottle baby out of the elements. For the first few days you will want to make sure the new baby is dry, warm, and comfortable. Plenty of warm straw bedding will do the trick or if extremely cold a heat lamp for extra coziness can be added.

Miniature Cattle

There are many reasons to raise miniature cattle.

Miniature cattle are unique and some can be very colorful cattle.

Excellent for people who enjoy caring for animals but want something besides a horse or dog.

Breeders who enjoy these animals usually prefer "the smaller the better" and most miniatures are under 36 inches tall with miniature zebu being about the smallest purebred breed as well as their crosses.

The small size of miniature cattle is not intimidating and it allows for easy caring for by even very young children. Many kids and their families enjoy animals but are intimidated the large animals. Miniature cattle offer a great opportunity for kids to learn responsibility by taking care of an animal that is easy to train and care for. Their small size makes bottle feeding easy for even very young kids. Taking care of an animal gives kids responsibility and they feel rewarded when they see their animal prosper. The small size makes the calves seem desirable for kids of any age.

Miniature cattle are made to order for home grown beef. With a national move toward healthy, hormone and chemically free food, miniature cattle have found a place. Beef type miniature cattle offer big options in a smaller package. These breeds and their crosses provide natural beef that can be raised and cared for at home with minimum equipment and feed expense. Miniature cattle are half the size of standard breeds but will still fill a freezer to about the right level for a small and growing family.

They are perfect for the small farm or ranch. Many small farms are less than 25 acres but need to be as self reliant as possible. Most small farm owners have employment outside the farm and need the small farm to be efficient and easily managed. Time does not afford them an opportunity for full scale farming or ranching. Miniature cattle are time and labor efficient. They are easier on the land, equipment, facilities, and people. Cattle being herd animals are much more content being raised in groups. Two or more will be much happier than one. They're docile, hearty, and easy calvers. Miniature cattle are low maintenance animals. Miniature cattle consume about one third the feed of full size cattle.

Miniature cattle are a more easily managed animal, docile and easier on you, your pastures and your fences. A more efficient animal on feed and pasture. They mature earlier. Good fertility and easy calving. Less birthing and maternal problems. Produce ideal amount of designer steaks for a typical family freezer for direct marketing or home use. Miniature cattle can be a wise tax deductible investment.

Interest in smaller, more efficient beef cattle is growing by leaps and bounds. The number of small hobbyists cattle breeders continues to grow and there are many miniature breeds available to fit their "back yard' sized farms. Miniature cattle are small in size, efficient in feed conversion, have a gentle disposition. All this makes them the ideal choice for locations with minimal acreage.

Purchase Considerations for Stocking a Small Beef Cattle Farm or Ranch

Condition:

If you purchase cattle to put on pasture try to avoid cattle with excess fat as they gain poorly for the first month. Cattle should be healthy but lean and avoid cattle that may not have performed well elsewhere. You may be able to purchase them for less money but they probably won't achieve an acceptable performance.

Health:

Does the animal look healthy?

Is it alert and bright eyed?

Is its breathing normal and does it move about vigorously?

Does it have a dull hair coat and look emaciated?

What has it been vaccinated for and when?

Frame Size:

Cattle with a small frame will finish at a light weight while cattle with a large frame will finish at a heavy weight. Cattle with different frame sizes require different feeding programs. Since you will want to manage your cattle as a group, purchase cattle that are uniform in frame size.

Breed:

In most situations frame and conformation are more important than breed in relation to cattle performance.

Some animals such as dairy type will require different management and sell in a different market category.

Animals with a high percentage of Brahman genetics do poorly in cold winter conditions.

The disposition of the cattle can be an important factor and is usually considered as being a breed characteristic. Avoid cattle that are high strung or aggressive.

Sources:

As with any purchase it is important that you get value

for your money. If you are uncertain about how to purchase a beef animal then it would be best to deal with someone who is ethical and understands this side of the business. This could include a family member, friend, neighbor, local farmer or County Agent. The idea is to not go into a purchase with little or no information or background.

Cattle can be purchased directly from beef producers with the price based on local market conditions. The local market is established primarily in commodity markets many miles away from where you live. These are then modified for each specific region of the country based on transportation costs to markets and local conditions. These local conditions could be such variables as abundance of feedstuffs, moisture conditions and supply and demand. Markets will change through the seasons and from year to year.

Within most areas there are also livestock auction markets in certain municipalities. Here livestock producers bring their animals and exhibit them through an auction ring and sold to the highest bidder. It is a system where potential buyers and sellers are brought together and a fair price established. In order to determine what may be fair, however, the potential buyer must have some idea of local market conditions and a predetermined animal type that they wish to purchase.

Market reports are provided on the radio and can be checked on a daily basis, along with local auction market prices on the Internet. Following the market for a couple of weeks before you purchase will help you insure that you are paying a fair price for your cattle. If you have done your homework it will assist you in purchasing at a fair price whether you purchase from a local auction or an individual.

Commercial market prices are quoted on the basis of the weight and sex of the animal sold. Generally there is little to nothing reported about the condition or quality of the animals. You may have to learn to judge quality and condition on your own or with the help of a trusted advisor.

The correct size for your enterprise: If you want stocker cattle to put on grass, calves that weigh less than 450 pounds may perform poorly on grass pasture. If cattle weigh over 750 pounds in the spring they will need to be on high quality pasture to make GRASS FINISHED BEEF or should not be fed on pasture. These larger cattle may need to be placed in a confined situation and fed a higher proportion of concentrate feeds, such as barley or corn. Make sure you have animals that fit your enterprise.

Beef Cattle Facilities and Equipment

Caring for animals on a small beef cattle farm does not require elaborate or expensive housing or facilities and equipment. Under most weather conditions, beef cattle do very well outside.

In wetter areas cows need a mud free area with protection from wind and rain. One method is to allow animals to have access to an open air pole shelter. In an enclosed building, proper ventilation is important to maintain good health.

Design your facilities to make your job easy and safe and to minimize your expenditure of time and labor. An effective working facility consists of a corral with a narrow alley, a head catch, and a squeeze chute.

The chute is needed for vaccinations, deworming, etc. The head catch is needed if you must aid a cow with calving. The corral and narrow alley help confine animals that need to be handled and driven into the chute or head catch.

Well-designed handling facilities help to minimize animal confusion and stress. Poorly designed facilities increase stress on the animals and may cause poor performance, which can affect meat quality. Use of electric prods is not recommended because they cause animals unnecessary pain and stress.

It is important to maintain the quality of feed. Store hay, straw, or silage and grains in a dry building free from rodents. Most all types of storage forages will lose nutritional value when exposed to direct sunlight. Hay put up wet or tto green loses feed value and palatability and presents a fire safety hazard due to combustion. Rodents can damage feed and spread disease.

Cattle feeders reduce waste and prevent the spread of many internal parasites and other cattle diseases. You can buy many kinds of manufactured feeders. Or, you can build them out of materials on hand.

An adequate, year round supply of clean, fresh water is basic to any successful cattle enterprise. Many types of water troughs are available from local feed or farm supply stores. You can recycle old barrels and bathtubs to make functional troughs; be sure to clean them thoroughly prior to use.

Pens, feedlots, and corrals should be located at a convenient distance from feed storage facilities. These areas should be well drained, with drainage moving away from feed storage, working facilities, and roads. It is important to make these areas accessible to tractors for easy feeding and cleaning.

Proper transportation is a must for your cattle. A one ton or 3/4 ton truck and trailer are convenient for any beef operation. A truck also is useful for transporting and dispersing hay.

One small to medium horsepower tractor, rotary pasture mower and hay moving equipment adds convenience to any beef cattle operation. It has been proven time and again that most failed beef cattle enterprises is due to over investment in heavy iron so one needs to be practicing caution in this area.

A Quick Look at Beef Cattle Parentage Confirmation and DNA

The beef cattle industry has for many years utilized parentage confirmation in their registered cattle. Experiences with this practice throughout the years has proven that parentage confirmation when in combination with a well run breeding program ensures more accurate pedigrees. More accurate pedigrees add value to the herd.

DNA samples are all subjected to an identical process. Each sample is assigned a unique ID to allow lab personnel to track the physical location and identify the DNA profile to be used in the parentage analysis. Many different sample types may be utilized for routine testing. Some of those are; blood, hair, semen, buccal swabs and blood FTA cards. Non-routine sample types include bone, teeth, saliva, dried blood, urine and feces.

DNA is extracted from the samples and microsatellite marker analysis begins with the PCR procedure. When a DNA profile, which provides alleles sizes for all microsatellite markers is obtained the parentage analysis is performed. In this process a computer program compares the DNA profile of the offspring to those of the presumed parents. A parentage analyst reviews the results and, if no problems exist, a report is finalized. If a listed parent or parents are excluded, additional analysis is performed including retest of samples and the possible use of additional DNA markers to confirm the exclusion.

The typical animal parentage case, species, includes a dam, offspring and one or more sires. Generally the identity of the dam is fairly certain. Parentage testing identifies individuals that, due to a specific combination of marker alleles, could qualify as a parent for a particular offspring. Accurate parentage testing requires breeders to identify possible parents since if considering a randomly selected large group of individuals there could be more than one that qualifies as a parent. A good application for animal parentage testing is verification that the dam is correct and which of the sires on a particular farm are the actual sire.

Finally, it is important to remember that while parentage exclusions are 100% accurate, parentage qualifications are not. The accuracy of most animal parentage tests is greater than 99% when both parents are included in the analysis and drops to around 95% when only one parent is included in the analysis. However, this accuracy will decrease when the potential parents are part of a large group of closely related animals. Again this is due to the fact that an animal closely related to an actual parent could possess marker alleles that would make it appear that animal is the correct parent. To prevent erroneous parentage qualifications breeders may submit samples from all possible parents when first requesting parentage verification. If more than one sire and one dam qualify as parents of an offspring the laboratory can then test with additional DNA markers to sort out the actual parents.

Breeding Beef Cattle

Artificial Insemination

Beef Cattle Artificial Insemination and Synchronization Information

Breeding For Marbling

Breeding For Marbling should result in an indirect improvement in tenderness, although the phenotypic relationship between marbling and tenderness is not especially high.

Bull Management For Yearling Bulls

Spring is most every cattle rancher's preferred or primary bull buying season. If you are like most of us, right or wrong, the yearling bulls seem to fit in better. This always seems to pose a need to learn the necessities of Bull **Management For Yearling Bulls.**

Bull Selection

Bull selection depends on the type of cows to be bred and the objectives of the producer.

Bull To Cow Ratio

How many cows should you allow per bull?

Herd Bull Status

Should every male calf born make it to "Herd Bull Status?" Information pertaining to "Marketing Bulls" for your consideration whether you are a buyer or seller.

Cattle Breeding

Modern cattle breeding practices today are still based largely on mass selection, supplemented by three other methods: pedigree selection, family selection, and progeny selection.

Genetics Terms

A Glossary of Beef Cattle Genetics Terms.

Tenderness Genetics

Beef Cattle Tenderness Genetics and Their Effects

Trichomoniasis

Trichomoniasis, or "trich," is a venereal disease of cattle caused by a protozoan parasite, Tritrichomonas foetus.

Beef Cattle Artificial Insemination

Beef producers know the best genetics are available as semen intended for artificial insemination (AI). Yet fewer than 10% of beef producers use the technology each year. There are many reasons that people do not use estrus synchronization and AI including labor and facilities and many still question if it is cost effective or not.

The use of estrus synchronization and artificial insemination can increase returns by increasing weaning weight (due to both age and genetics), by raising the market price with a more uniform calf crop, and by improving herd productivity with higher quality replacement heifers. They can also reduce costs because fewer bulls are needed and less labor is required during a more concentrated and predictable calving season.

On the other hand, fewer bulls mean fewer bulls available to sell as culls — a reduction in potential income. The need for synchronization products, labor, technicians and perhaps facilities will also increase the cost associated with estrus synchronization and artificial insemination.

When all these impacts are compiled, however, the costs of pregnancy aren't significantly different between natural service and estrus synchronization and AI. Of course, if labor is high, if semen costs are excessive, or if conception rate to AI is low, the cost per pregnancy can dramatically increase. The benefits of estrus synchronization and artificial insemination will depend greatly on the management of a beef herd. A herd with adequate nutrition, facilities and labor may benefit greatly while a herd lacking in any of those areas may not benefit at all. Careful consideration and proper planning are crucial when implementing these technologies but for many farms, they may be beneficial.

Commercial producers who specialize in maternal or terminal trait selection and who adopt synchronized breeding with artificial insemination can make rapid genetic progress.

Breeding For Marbling To Improve Tenderness

Breeding For Marbling should result in an indirect improvement in tenderness, although the phenotypic relationship between marbling and tenderness is not especially high. Increased marbling results in a dilution effect on the connective tissue (collagen) in meat and provides lubrication in the chewing process, both of which aid in the improvement of tenderness. Increased marbling is most important when meat is cooked to relatively high endpoint temperatures. Several research studies have shown that the risks of having steaks of undesirable tenderness increase significantly as USDA quality grades decrease from Prime to Choice to Select to Standard.

Breeders of several purebred breeds have been selecting for increased marbling through progeny testing of sires and(or) ultrasound evaluation of progeny of sires. Some studies have shown that the genetic correlation between marbling and tenderness tends to be higher than the phenotypic correlation.

Because of its high level of heritability (38 %), progress can and has already been made by selecting for increased marbling. Several breed associations are now using ultrasound information obtained by certified technicians and images interpreted by Iowa State University for development of EPDs for marbling as well as ribeye area and fat thickness. Using beef breeds that are noted for high marbling in crossbreeding programs generally results in meat that has a desirable level of marbling. Current pricing systems for carcasses and meat reward higher levels of marbling; therefore, the economic incentive for increased marbling likely will continue to be important in the future.

We should point out the relationship between marbling and percentage of meat yield is antagonistic. In other words, as marbling increases, percentage of meat yield generally decreases, unless both traits are selected for simultaneously. We also should reemphasize that the phenotypic relationship between marbling and tenderness is not especially high, although favorable. Consequently, some cattle with relatively high marbling will produce meat that is unacceptable in tenderness, and some cattle with low levels of marbling will produce meat that is very desirable in tenderness. The ideal situation would be to select directly for tenderness (or against toughness) and simultaneously select for increased marbling and improved percentage of meat yield. However, direct selection for tenderness (or against toughness) has not been feasible because tenderness can be evaluated only on cooked meat obtained from progeny groups of cattle. Even when tenderness information is obtained, it has not been available in "producer friendly" tenderness EPDs.

Producing beef of desirable tenderness requires utilizing beef cattle breeds or composites that are known for producing meat of acceptable tenderness, selecting for a calm temperament, selecting for tenderness within breeds, utilizing optimum management for different biological types, proper handling of finished cattle from the feedlot to the processing plant, utilizing optimum postmortem technology for carcasses and meat, and utilizing optimum cooking procedures. Of course, the beef cattle industry can control only the first three or four of these important variables.

Commercial cattlemen first should utilize breeds in their production system that match the environment and feed resources, but also must give considerable attention to utilizing those breeds that are known to produce meat of acceptable tenderness. When EPDs become available, seedstock producers should breed for improved tenderness (or against toughness) as well as marbling and desirable carcass cutability, so that commercial cattlemen can select sires within breeds to improve tenderness and meet market demands for marbling and carcass cutability.

When other technologies are proven accurate and reliable, such as testing for DNA tenderness markers, seedstock producers can make even more progress in improving tenderness, both from the standpoint of selecting sires earlier and from the standpoint of selecting among more sires.

Commercial cattlemen must castrate bulls at a young age, match the appropriate nutritional regimen with the type of cattle they are producing, feed cattle a high grain diet at least 100 days, utilize growth promotants according to manufacturers' recommendations, slaughter cattle at an optimum endpoint for their biological type, and handle cattle in a way to minimize excitement and stress.

The beef industry also must utilize technology and management to optimize tenderness, and the end users of beef must cook it properly. When both genetic selection and optimum management are utilized, tenderness of beef can be improved significantly, and beef's market share likely will increase.

Bull Selection For The Beef Cattle Herd

Bull selection depends on the type of cows to be bred and the objectives of the producer. The best bull for one herd will not necessarily be a good choice for another herd. Following are three examples of how the herd situation can affect bull selection.

Beef Cattle Breeder #1 has a small herd of crossbred cows. He works in town during the day and has a limited amount of time to spend with the cattle. He has at best average pastures with limited facilities and needs to use the same bull on both heifers and mature cows. For producer 1, calving ease would be of major importance, so low birth weight EPDs would be necessary. This producer may have to accept somewhat lower weaning and yearling weight EPDs to find a low birth weight bull. With his pasture situation, average milk to moderately low milk production would be acceptable. Producer 1 would want to avoid extremes in frame. With limited facilities, disposition would also be a major consideration.

Beef Cattle Breeder #2 has an average size herd of medium frame crossbred cattle that works well under his management situation. He has good pastures and needs a bull to breed to mature cows in a rotational crossbreeding program. Producer 2 would balance moderate birth weight EPDs against higher weaning and yearling EPDs. He would be willing to accept somewhat higher birth weight than Producer 1 in order to get higher weaning and yearling EPDs. With good pastures, moderately high milk EPDs may be desirable. Since his cows are working well in their environment, a bull of similar frame and muscle would be chosen.

Beef Cattle Breeder #3 has a large herd of medium frame cattle and plans to breed some of his mature cows to a terminal sire. All of these calves will be placed in the feedlot. Producer 3 will want to maximize weaning and yearling weight EPDs. He will have a higher tolerance for birth weight than either Producer 1 or 2, but he will still avoid bulls with extremely high birth weight EPDs. Since all heifers are going into the feedlot, milk EPDs are not a factor. A larger framed bull may be desirable to produce a specific carcass weight. A heavy muscled bull would also be desirable.

In the above examples, these producers with three

different herds and objectives would choose three different bulls. Setting goals and evaluating the cow herd are important first steps in bull selection.

Bull Management For Yearling Bulls

Spring is most every cattle rancher's preferred or primary bull buying season. If you are like most of us, right or wrong, the yearling bulls seem to fit in better.This always seems to pose a need to learn the necessities of Bull Management For Yearling Bulls.

You will need to spend time studying performance information, pedigrees and other pertinent information as sire selection is the most important tool for making genetic progress in your herd. Of equal importance is the care and management of the newly acquired bull. Proper management and nutrition are essential for the bull to perform satisfactorily during the breeding season. With most new herd sires purchased as yearling bulls, management prior to, during, and after the first breeding season is particularly important.

Management Prior to the Breeding Season

Many newly purchased yearling bulls will have been

provided a high plane of nutrition. The energy level of the diet should gradually be reduced to prevent excessive fat deposition. The reduction in energy may be accomplished through restricting intake of high energy grain supplements, in conjunction with supplying a total diet lower in energy content (primarily forage). Young bulls should be managed to be a body condition score 6 at turn out. This will give the bull adequate reserves of energy for use during the breeding season. Yearling bulls can be expected to lose 100 pounds or more during the course of the breeding season.

Acquiring a new yearling bull at least 60 to 90 days prior to the breeding season is critical from several aspects. First, this leaves ample time for the new bull to get adjusted to the feed and environment of his new home. Secondly, adequate exercise, in combination with a proper nutritional program, is essential to "harden" him up prior to the breeding season. A facility for the newly acquired bull that allows for ample exercise will help create bulls that are physically fit for the breeding season. The nutrition of the bull will be dependent on body condition. Yearling bulls are still growing and developing, and should be targeted to gain 2.0 to 2.5 pounds per day from a year of age through the breeding season. Bulls weighing approximately 1200 pounds will consume 25 to 30 pounds of dry matter per day. This intake may consist of high quality pasture plus 12 lbs corn, grass legume hay plus 12 lbs corn, or 80 lbs corn silage plus 2 lbs protein supplement. Provide adequate clean water, and a complete mineral free choice.

Prior to the breeding season, all bulls should receive breeding soundness exams (BSE) to assure fertility. All bulls that are to be used should have a BSE annually. Because a variety of factors may affect bull fertility, it may be advisable to re-test young bulls before the breeding season even if it has only been a few months since their pre sale BSE.

Management During the Breeding Season

The breeding season should be kept to a maximum of 60 days for young bulls. This will prevent over-use of the bull, severe weight loss and reduced libido. Severe weight loss may impair future growth and development of the young bull, and reduce his lifetime usefulness. When practical, supplementary feeding young bulls during the breeding season will reduce excessive weight loss.

In single sire situations, young bulls can normally be expected to breed a number of females approximately equal to their age in months. Using this rule of thumb, a newly purchased bull that is 18 months of age could be placed with 18 cows or heifers. Bulls used together in multiple sire breeding pastures should be of similar age and size. Young bulls cannot compete with older bulls in the same breeding pasture. A common practice is to rotate bulls among different breeding pastures every 21 to 28 days. This practice decreases the breeding pressure on a single bull. Some producers use older bulls early in the breeding season, and then replace them with young bulls. The appropriate bull to female ratio will vary from one operation to the next based on bull age, condition, fertility, and libido, as well as size of the breeding pasture, available forage supply, length of the breeding season and number of bulls with a group of cows.

All bulls should be observed closely to monitor their breeding behavior and libido to ensure they are servicing and settling cows. Additionally, observe the cowherd to monitor their estrous cycles. Many females coming back into heat may be the result of an infertile or subfertile bull. All bulls should be monitored for injury or lameness that may compromise their breeding capability.

Management After the Breeding Season

Young bulls require a relatively high plane of nutrition following the breeding season to replenish body condition and meet demands for continued growth. Yearling bulls should be maintained in a separate lot from mature bulls, so these additional nutritional requirements can be provided. Body condition and projected mature size of the bull will determine his nutrient requirements during the months following the breeding season and until next breeding season. Bulls should be kept away from cows in an isolated facility or pasture after the breeding season. In the winter months, provide cover from extreme weather that may cause frostbite to the scrotum resulting in decreased fertility.

All herd bulls should receive breeding soundness exams (BSE) to assure fertility on an annual basis. Assess the bull battery well in advance of the breeding season, so that new herd sires can be acquired in a timely fashion.

Bull To Cow Ratio

Number of cows to expect a bull to cover in one

breeding season.

The three major goals of any breeding season should be to: get the cows settled as early in the breeding season as possible; get them bred to the bulls with the highest possible genetic worth; and achieve both as economically as possible, by getting the cows bred with the fewest possible bulls. Defining the optimum bull to female ratio is important to a successful breeding season. However, no one ratio is optimal for all ranches or small herd operations. The number of bulls required to adequately cover the breeding females is related to many factors. Some of those factors are; Distribution of the breeding females, Terrain, Water availability, Carrying capacity--feed intensity, Pasture adaptation and Pasture size.

Factors more related directly to the bull may be; Age, Condition, Mating ability, Libido, Fertility, Sperm reserve, Social behavior and Injury.

Factors related to or considered as Management Decisions include; Length of breeding season, Reproductive diseases, Breeding intensity and
Amount of observation.

Most of these factors must be considered to define the optimum bull to cow ratio in a beef cattle operation.

Proper management during the breeding season should result in each cow being bred by a single fertile bull each time she is in estrus. Bull overlap (more than one bull breeding a cow in heat) is not desirable, primarily because it does not enhance pregnancy rates. Disadvantages of bull overlap are increased risk of bull injury (through competition for estrous females), additional pressure from social dominance and the extra costs incurred by purchasing and maintaining more bulls.

Bull overlap can be decreased by eliminating bull congregation within breeding pastures. This can be achieved by dividing the breeding herd into separate pastures or by using pastures that have natural barriers that reduce mixing of breeding groups. In addition, riders can be used to keep bulls well distributed among breeding groups.

These large cow to bull ratios can reduce bull costs on very large ranches with minimal risk. On a small 50 to 100 cow operation, using just one bull that happens to undergo an injury or disease could spell disaster for an entire calf crop.

Recommendations for smaller herds that will utilize only one bull per pasture may need to be more conservative.

A time honored rule-of-thumb is to place about the same number of cows or heifers with a young bull as his age is in months.

For instance a bull that is 14 months old going into his first breeding season should be expected to breed 14 or 15 cows; whereas as a two-year old bull may be placed with 20 - 25 cows. Mature bulls that have been examined by a veterinarian and have passed a breeding soundness exam can be placed with 25 - 35 cows and normally give good results.

From Bull Calf To Herd Bull Status

Information pertaining to "Marketing Bulls" for your consideration whether you are a buyer or seller.

Should every male calf born make it to "Herd Bull Status?"

How many cows are in the average size breeding herd? On average each year half of the calves will be bulls. Even if the herd is the "Best of Breed" will there be a premium market for all those bull calves as herd bulls?

Have you thought about how the recommended "Bull To Cow Ratio" and "Bull Culling Age" might figure into developing a program for marketing herd bulls?

College research says the standard recommendation for a bull-to-cow ratio is 1 bull to each 25 cows. This is pretty typical in the real world although it makes allowance for sub-standard bulls. Research has shown that this ratio can under-utilize bull power. Under-utilization of bull power with a 1 to 25 ratio is especially true in situations where the stocking density is high due to an abundance of high quality native forage, and when the bull is highly fertile. Libido and serving capacity of bulls are helpful components to assess in order to optimize the bull to female ratio.

College research says age is a major consideration when making culling decisions for beef bulls. Semen quality begins to decline after age 6 and this is also about the same age when mature bulls lose their social dominance rank to younger more aggressive bulls. If a bull over age 7 has exceptional value it is recommended to utilize that bull in single-sire pastures, or by hand mating, and ensure that he passes a thorough breeding soundness exam before each breeding season. Other factors that should be considered when making culling decisions are vision, conformation and disposition. Also bulls that produce poor performing calves should be ear marked for culling.

Now do a quick and easy math exercise. Keep it simple and use 1 bull for each 20 cows and only use him for 5 years.

Are you beginning to see the quality needed for a true "Herd Bull Prospect?"

It appears like a breeder with 20 cows will be a prospective bull buyer once each 5 years. On average a seed stock herd of 20 cows will produce 50 bull calves in 5 years. From this perspective we begin to get a clearer picture into selection and marketing bulls for breeding purposes?

Cattle Breeding

Modern cattle breeding practices today are still based largely on mass selection, supplemented by three other methods: pedigree selection, family selection, and progeny selection.

Pedigree selection focuses on the quality of the ancestors rather than of the individual. Pedigree selection is useful in evaluating young animals whose phenotypes are not fully developed, and in selecting for traits that are known to have high heritability. However, pedigree selection is a slow process.

Family selection, based on analyzing the qualities of relatives, is faster. Family selection is often used in conjunction with individual selection, and it is valuable in estimating sex limited traits in selecting the males from which to breed.

Progeny selection involves selecting individuals based on the records of their progeny. Like family selection, it is useful when selecting for such sex limited traits as milk yields in the progeny of a bull and traits with low or uncertain heritability. However, progeny selection is a slow process because it requires waiting for one generation or more to determine the quality of a given individual's offspring.

Since the mid 18th century, cattle breeders have combined various methods of selection with inbreeding and outbreeding of stocks.

Inbreeding involves crosses between closely related individuals. To fix or intensify a particular trait, herds or flocks are subdivided into smaller groups and intensively inbred for several generations. To increase vigor and avoid the accumulation of unwanted traits, individuals from these inbred stocks are then outbred, or crossed with members of other stocks.

Outbreeding increases variability and produces new combinations of traits. Increasingly in the 20th century, as methods for freezing and storing sperm have been perfected, both inbreeding and outbreeding have been carried out by artificial insemination.

Embryo selection is another method by which the breeder can increase desired traits in a population. In this method, fertility hormones are given to females that carry selected characteristics. Once the eggs have been fertilized, they are taken from the selected females and implanted in other females that carry them through the gestation period and then give birth. Embryo transfer is used less frequently than artificial insemination because it is more complicated and more expensive.

Beef Cattle Tenderness Genetics and Their Effects

Effects of Genetics on Tenderness

The extensive Germ Plasm Evaluation research project at the U. S. Meat Animal Research Center, Clay Center, Nebraska, demonstrated that significant differences in tenderness of steaks occurred between cattle sired by Bos nvolv breeds and those sired by Bos indicus breeds when mated to Hereford and Angus cows. Mean tenderness differences among Bos nvolv-sired cattle when mated to Angus or Hereford dams were small, even though there were significant sire breed differences in marbling. However, in the extensive Germ Plasm Utilization research project at the U.S. Meat Animal Research Center involving several pure breeds of cattle, significant tenderness differences occurred among purebred Bos nvolv cattle. Average tenderness for some purebreds was considered marginally unacceptable, and marbling score was correlated highly with the tenderness differences among breeds. Yet, when three composite breeds were formed from the purebreds to balance favorable carcass composition and meat palatability, tenderness of longissimus steaks did not differ.

Reviews of published literature on tenderness genetics show that the heritability of Warner-Bratzler shear force is moderately high (29 %). A few studies have shown that the heritability of calpastatin activity, the inhibitor to the calpain enzyme system involved in postmortem tenderization, is quite high (40-70 %). Numerous studies have shown that marbling, one of the factors that affects tenderness, is also high in heritability (38 %). These levels of heritability suggest that progress could be made through selection, if the traits could be measured easily. The advantages of genetic selection are that it is cumulative and permanent as compared to management practices. However, selecting for tenderness and other palatability traits has been difficult because of the coordination, time, and expense required in obtaining steaks from meat processing plants on a routine basis. Furthermore, generally only university or government research labs have the capability to accurately measure tenderness genetics and their effects.

Expected Progeny Differences (EPD's) have become

"user friendly" tools for cattlemen to use in selecting for numerous production traits, but as of December, 2000, only one cattle breed association had EPD's for Warner-Bratzler shear force and none had EPD's for sensory evaluated tenderness or other palatability traits. In addition, not much economic incentive has existed in the past for seedstock producers to select for tenderness. Therefore, selection for tenderness has not been practiced. Recent surveys have demonstrated that consumers are willing to pay for known or guaranteed tenderness and some producers of branded products are showing interest in marketing beef with guaranteed tenderness. Consequently, the economic incentive to select for tenderness may now exist.

Breed Differences in Tenderness

Considerable research data are available that show some breed differences in longissimus tenderness among purebred Bos nvolv cattle, but these differences can be minimized by including at least 25% "British""breeding in crossbreeding programs. Crosses of most "Continental" with typical "British" breeds produce meat that generally is very acceptable in average tenderness, although variability still exists among animals. Several the "composite breeds" include at least 25% "British" breeding, and mean tenderness generally is very acceptable in them.

Several studies have shown that as the percentage of Bos indicus breeding increases, tenderness decreases almost linearly. Research data suggest that the percentage of Bos nvolv "British" breeding should be at least 62.5% (5/8) in Bos indicus x Bos nvolv crosses in order to provide an acceptable average level of tenderness. Thus, "composites" that consist of 5/8 British Bos nvolv origins x 3/8 Bos indicus breeding generally provide an acceptable level of tenderness. However, considerable variability can still exist, and some cattle will produce meat that is unacceptable in tenderness.

Breeding For Marbling should result in an indirect improvement in tenderness, although the phenotypic relationship between marbling and tenderness is not especially high. Increased marbling results in a dilution effect on the connective tissue (collagen) in meat and provides lubrication in the chewing process, both of which aid in the improvement of tenderness. Increased marbling is most important when meat is cooked to relatively high endpoint temperatures. Several research studies have shown that the risks of having steaks of undesirable tenderness increase significantly as USDA quality grades decrease from Prime to Choice to Select to Standard. Breeders of several purebred breeds have been selecting for increased marbling through progeny testing of sires and(or) ultrasound evaluation of progeny of sires. Some studies have shown that the genetic correlation between marbling and tenderness tends to be higher than the phenotypic correlation.

Because of its high level of heritability (38 %), progress can and has already been made by selecting for increased marbling. Several breed associations are now using ultrasound information obtained by certified technicians and images interpreted by Iowa State University for development of EPDs for marbling as well as ribeye area and fat thickness. Using beef breeds that are noted for high marbling in crossbreeding programs generally results in meat that has a desirable level of marbling. Current pricing systems for carcasses and meat reward higher levels of marbling; therefore, the economic incentive for increased marbling likely will continue to be important in the future.

We should point out the relationship between marbling and percentage of meat yield is antagonistic. In other words, as marbling increases, percentage of meat yield generally decreases, unless both traits are selected for simultaneously. We also should reemphasize that the phenotypic relationship between marbling and tenderness is not especially high, although favorable. Consequently, some cattle with relatively high marbling will produce meat that is unacceptable in tenderness, and some cattle with low levels of marbling will produce meat that is very desirable in tenderness. The ideal situation would be to select directly for tenderness (or against toughness) and simultaneously select for increased marbling and improved percentage of meat yield. However, direct selection for tenderness (or against toughness) has not been feasible because tenderness can be evaluated only on cooked meat obtained from progeny groups of cattle. Even when tenderness information is obtained, it has not been available in "producer friendly" tenderness EPDs.

Producing beef of desirable tenderness requires utilizing beef cattle breeds or composites that are known for producing meat of acceptable tenderness, selecting for a calm temperament, selecting for tenderness within breeds, utilizing optimum management for different biological types, proper handling of finished cattle from the feedlot to the processing plant, utilizing optimum postmortem technology for carcasses and meat, and utilizing optimum cooking procedures. Of course, the beef cattle industry can control only the first three or four of these important variables.

Commercial cattlemen first should utilize breeds in their production system that match the environment and feed resources, but also must give considerable attention to utilizing those breeds that are known to produce meat of acceptable tenderness. When EPDs become available, seedstock producers should breed for improved tenderness (or against toughness) as well as marbling and desirable carcass cutability, so that commercial cattlemen can select sires within breeds to improve tenderness and meet market demands for marbling and carcass cutability.

When other technologies are proven accurate and reliable, such as testing for DNA tenderness markers, seedstock producers can make even more progress in improving tenderness, both from the standpoint of selecting sires earlier and from the standpoint of selecting among more sires.

Commercial cattlemen must castrate bulls at a young age, match the appropriate nutritional regimen with the type of cattle they are producing, feed cattle a high grain diet at least 100 days, utilize growth promotants according to manufacturers' recommendations, slaughter cattle at an optimum endpoint for their biological type, and handle cattle in a way to minimize excitement and stress.

The beef industry also must utilize technology and management to optimize tenderness, and the end users of beef must cook it properly. When both genetic selection and optimum management are utilized, tenderness of beef can be improved significantly, and beef's market share likely will increase.

Beef Cattle Genetics Terms

A Glossary of Beef Cattle Genetics Terms

Adenine:

One of the four bases in DNA that make up the letters ATGC, adenine is the "A". The others are guanine, cytosine, and thymine. Adenine always pairs with thymine.

Allele:

The various possible forms of a gene. A single allele for each locus (location on a chromosome) is inherited from each parent. Different alleles produce variation in inherited characteristics such as coat color. In an individual, one form of the allele (the dominant one) may be expressed more than another form (the recessive one). When an individual has two identical alleles for the same trait, (AA, bb, etc.), they are homozygous. Two contrasting alleles of the same trait (Aa, Bb, etc.) are heterozygous.

Base Pair:

Two bases which form a "rung of the DNA ladder." A DNA nucleotide is made of a molecule of sugar, a molecule of phosphoric acid, and a molecule called a base. The bases are the "letters" that spell out the genetic code. In DNA, the code letters are A, T, G, and C, which stand for the chemicals adenine, thymine, guanine, and cytosine, respectively. In base pairing, adenine always pairs with thymine, and guanine always pairs with cytosine.

Cell:

The basic unit of any living organism. It is a small, watery, compartment filled with chemicals and a complete copy of the organism's genome.

Chromosome:

The structure in the cell nucleus that stores and transmits genetic information in the form of DNA. Each parent contributes one chromosome to each pair, so offspring get half of their chromosomes from their dam and half from their sires.

Cytosine:

One of the four bases in DNA that make up the letters ATGC, cytosine is the "C".

The others are adenine, guanine, and thymine. Cytosine always pairs with guanine

DNA

(Deoxyribonucleic Acid) The chemical inside the nucleus of a cell that carries the genetic instructions for making living organisms. It is the molecule that encodes genetic information.

DNA replication:

The process by which the DNA double helix unwinds and makes an exact copy of itself.

Dominant:

A gene that almost always results in a specific physical characteristic. Only one copy the gene is needed in order for the trait to appear.

Double Helix:

The structural arrangement of DNA, which looks something like an immensely long
ladder twisted into a helix, or coil.

Environment:

Factors that influence the expression of genes such as nutrition, disease, weather, management, etc.

Gene:

The functional and physical unit of heredity passed from parent to offspring.

Genotype:

The genetic identity of an individual as distinguished from its physical appearance
(phenotype).

Gene Mapping:

Determining the relative positions of genes on a chromosome and the distance between them.

Genetic Marker:

Known sequence believed to be near actual genes and statistically associated with phenotype. Markers are used to find genes, but can be used in some cases for selection before the gene is known. The closer the marker is to the gene, the more consistent the effect.

Genome:

All the genetic material in the chromosomes of a particular organism.

Genotype:

The genetic identity of an individual that does not show as outward characteristics.

Guanine:

One of the four bases in DNA that make up the letters ATGC, guanine is the "G". The others are adenine, cytosine, and thymine. Guanine always pairs with cytosine. Heterozygous: Possessing two different forms of a particular gene, one inherited from each parent.

Homozygous:

Possessing two identical forms of a particular gene, one inherited from each parent.
Locus: The place on a chromosome where a specific gene is located, a kind of address for the gene.

Mendelian Inheritance:

Manner in which genes and traits are passed from parents to offspring.

Microsatellite:

Repetitive stretches of short sequences of DNA used as genetic markers to track inheritance in families.

Natural Variation:

A permanent structural alteration in DNA. In most cases, DNA changes either have no effect or cause harm, but occasionally a mutation can improve an organism's chance of surviving and passing the beneficial change on to its descendants.

Nucleus:

The central cell structure that houses the chromosomes.

Nucleotides:

One of the structural components, or building blocks, of DNA. A nucleotide consists of a base (one of four chemicals: adenine, thymine, guanine, and cytosine) plus a molecule of sugar and one of phosphoric acid.

Phenotype:

The observable traits or characteristics of an organism, for example hair color, weight, or the presence or absence of a disease. Phenotypic traits are not necessarily genetic and results from the interaction of genotype and the environment.

Quantitative Trait Loci (QTL):

The location on the chromosome that contains a gene or genes affecting economically important quantitative traits. Recessive: A trait that appears only in animals who have received two copies of a non-dominate gene, one from each parent.

Single Nucleotide Polymorphisms (SNPs):

Pronounced "snip" This is a functional variation that occurs at a specific point in the DNA – on one of the rungs of the DNA ladder called nucleotides. It is predictable, and its occurrence in the population cannot be attributed to recurrent random variation alone. Thus, it is called a Stable Variant Allele.

Thymine:

One of the four bases in DNA that make up the letters ATGC, thymine is the "T". The others are adenine, guanine, and cytosine. Thymine always pairs with adenine.

Calving Time

Calving and When To Help A Cow

Learning when to help a cow during calving may be one of the most profitable practices you can acquire.

Research has shown that up to 10 percent of all calves born in beef cattle herds in the United States are deceased at or soon after birth. With half of those deaths being due to calving difficulty, also referred to as dystocia. In the beef cattle industry this causes millions of dollar losses annually and is second only to losses from failing to conceive.

Calving difficulty can be expected to be more pronounced when mating a larger continental type of bull to a British breed cow. You should also be aware of possible increased calving problems in a purebred breed if you are inclined to mate genetically large bulls to purebred cows that are average in size.

You should always consult with your veterinarian for further information or assistance when in doubt.

Beef Cattle Calving Assistance

A knowledgeable beef cattle breeder will always be ready and prepared for calving assistance when the need arises.

Normal delivery in cattle should be completed within 2 hours after the water sac appears. If prolonged, the calf may be born dead or in a weakened condition. Since timing is vital to providing proper assistance, frequent observations are a must. Assisted deliveries should not be attempted without proper preparation of facilities and equipment. A clean, well-lighted maternity pen and clean pulling chains and equipment are desirable to reduce bacterial contamination.

It is always best to first check with your veterinarian for advice on when to assist the cow alone and when to call him. Since cervical dilation is completed in Stage 2, assistance can be given too early. However, since final dilation is quite rapid, assistance is often given too late, which is much more serious.

Cleanliness cannot be overemphasized. Introduction of bacteria by equipment or arms of the person assisting with the calving may reduce fertility of the cow by delaying return to estrus and lowering conception. Equipment needs are two clean buckets, soap (for cleaning the cow), disinfectant, obstetrical lubricant, paper towels, calving chains and handles and plastic sleeves. Have water in both buckets -- disinfectant is added to the second bucket. Place the calving chains and handles in the disinfectant solution.

Restrain the cow with head catch or halter. Tie the tail with light twine to the neck of the cow. Scrub the perineal area (around the anus and vulva) and the tail with soapy water. Pour water from the bucket to rinse the area. Do not dip dirty towels back into the bucket. When the area is clean, dry with paper towels. Use the remainder of the water in the first bucket to wash your hands and arms. If possible use plastic sleeves on initial examination. This may prevent contact with abortion-causing organisms that can infect humans. Apply an obstetrical lubricant to the sleeves. If extensive manipulation of the fetus is needed, the gloves may be removed since they tear easily.

Beef Cattle Calving Assistance Explained

There is a lot to be considered in any attempt to put a subject like "Calving Assistance Explained" in words. Many of those considerations are included here for your information and education.

Some Calving Assistance Explanations

1. After observing a delay in delivery, a pelvic examination should be done to determine the extent of cervical dilation. It should be dilated enough to allow easy passage of the fetus.

2. Determine the position of the fetus (Figures 1 and 2). If it is in an abnormal position, experience and judgment must be used to determine if a correction can be made or if professional help should be summoned.

3. Examine the size of the calf relative to the birth canal. A large calf forced through a small pelvic opening may result in death of the calf and injury (including paralysis) to the cow. If this examination is made when the head and front feet are still in the birth canal, the opportunity for a successful caesarean section exists.

4. If the examination indicates a dry fetus and birth canal, additional lubrication is needed. Use a commercial obstetrical lubricant (methyl-cellulose product) or

petrolatum (Vaseline®). Do not use soap as it is irritating to the vaginal membranes, causes inflammation and swelling of the reproductive tract and can result in delayed return to estrus and lower conception rates.

5. Attach the obstetrical (pulling) chains to the front legs of the calf, placing the loop of each chain around each leg. Placement of the chains should be around the pastern (below the dewclaw and above the hooves) with the looped chain on top of the hooves. Careful attention to this placement when pulling on the chains will generally result in the least amount of damage to the calf. If the chains are allowed to become slack and/or excessive force is applied, the chain may damage the hooves. Placing the chains above the fetlocks (above the dewclaws) with a half-hitch around the pastern can result in broken front leg(s).

6. Attach the obstetrical handles and pull gently, making sure the chains have not slipped. Although some calves can be delivered by pulling both legs evenly, it's usually best to alternately pull on one leg and then the other a few inches at a time. Once the legs are "walked out" in this manner, the shoulders are allowed to pass through the pelvic opening one at a time. If the shoulders should happen to "lock" at the opening, apply traction to the calf's head by attaching a chain around the poll and through the mouth.

This traction will reduce compaction of the head against the sacrum (top of the birth canal) and reduce the dimensions of the shoulder and chest region.

7. The chance of uterine or cervical lacerations and tears is greatest when the calf's head and shoulders come through the birth canal. Such damage may lead to infections and future reproductive problems. Since pressure dilates the birth canal, damage can usually be prevented if traction is applied gradually. Gradual application of traction also helps prevent damage to the cow if assistance happens to be given too early, because very slow traction will not interfere with normal dilation of the cervix.

8. Once the head and shoulders are exposed, rotate the calf a quarter of a turn to aid in the hips entering the pelvic canal. If this does not allow delivery, pull the calf downward at a 45-degree angle, or nearly parallel with the rear legs of the cow.

9. "Hip lock" can be a problem serious enough to cause loss of the calf. If it happens in a cow lying down, push the fetus back a short distance and rotate the calf a quarter turn, then apply traction to the front legs in a direction toward the cow's flank or side. This rotates the calf enough so one hip bone goes through the pelvic opening ahead of the other. If you are unable to repel or rotate the calf, place the

calf's legs between the cow's hind legs and pull forward. If delivery is delayed, make sure the calf begins breathing normally as the umbilical cord will be pinched closed.

10. All posterior (rear feet first) presentations should be considered an emergency, because the umbilical cord is pinched between the fetus and pelvis early in the delivery. This means blood circulation is slowed, and the fetus may die or sustain brain damage unless delivery is rapid.

11. Attach the obstetrical chains above the fetlock joint and be sure the birth canal is adequately lubricated, since extraction is against the normal direction of hair growth. A posterior delivery is usually eased by alternating traction on the rear legs and by rotating the fetus about a quarter of a turn to take advantage of the greatest diameter of the cow's pelvis. If delivery proves extremely difficult, a caesarean section is probably necessary and should not be delayed.

12. Only an experienced herdsman or veterinarian should use mechanical calf pullers. If used incorrectly, permanent damage can occur to both calf and cow.

13. Correcting abnormal presentations other than a leg or head turned back usually requires professional help. For instance, a fetus that is upside down may be in that position because the uterus or fetus is rotated.

Beef Cattle Calving Problems - Some Causes

About 80 percent of all calves lost at birth are anatomically normal. Most of them die because of injuries or suffocation resulting from difficult or delayed parturition (calving). Factors contributing to calving difficulty usually fall into three main categories -- calf effects, cow effects and fetal position at birth.

Calf effects

Heavy birth weights account for most of the problems related to the calf. Birth weights are influenced by breed of the sire, bull within a breed, sex of the calf, age of the cow and, to a slight degree, nutrition of the cow. Shape of the calf may also have a small effect.

Cow effects

Several factors associated with the cow influence dystocia, the major ones being her age and pelvic size.

Cow Age

First-calf heifers require more assistance in calving than do cows, because they are usually structurally smaller.

Pelvic area

Pelvic area (birth canal) increases as the female develops to maturity. Thus, a higher proportion of calving difficulty in 2- or 3-year-old cows is due to smaller pelvic openings. Heifers and cows with small pelvic areas are likely to require assistance at calving. However, even heifers with a large pelvic area may need help delivering large calves.

The calf's birth weight and cow's pelvic area have a combined effect on dystocia. Many heifers giving birth to calves weighing more than 80 pounds will have difficulty, even if they have large pelvic areas. Two-year-old heifers tend to have either a pelvis too small or a calf too large to allow them to deliver without assistance. Therefore, calving problems could be reduced by decreasing birth weight through bull selection and/or increasing pelvic area by selecting the larger, more growthy heifers.

Fetal position at birth

Occasionally up to about 5 percent of the calves at birth are in abnormal positions, such as forelegs or head turned back, breech, rear end position, sideways or rotated, etc. This requires the assistance of a veterinarian or an experienced herdsman to position the fetus correctly prior to delivery. If fetal position cannot be corrected, the veterinarian may have to perform a caesarean section.

Beef Cattle Calving Stages

We normally think of beef cattle calving stages to be divided into three general stages, preparatory, fetal expulsion and expulsion of the placenta or afterbirth. The time interval of each stage varies among types and breeds of beef cattle and among individuals of the same breed. Although the exact stimulus that initiates parturition is unknown, it does involve hormonal changes in both the cow and fetus as well as mechanical and neural stimulation in the uterus.

A general understanding of the birth process is important to proper calving assistance.

Stage 1

Preparatory (2 to 6 hours). During pregnancy, the fetal calf is normally on its back. Just prior to labor, it rotates to an upright position with its forelegs and head pointed toward the birth canal. This position provides the least resistance during birth. Toward the end of gestation, the muscular lining of the dam's uterus increases in size, which aids in delivery.

In the preparatory stage, the cervix dilates and rhythmic contractions of the uterus begin. Initially, contractions occur at about 15-minute intervals. As labor progresses, they become more frequent until they occur every few minutes. These contractions begin at the back of the uterine horn and continue toward the cervix, forcing the fetus outward. Any unusual disturbance or stress during this period, such as excitement, may inhibit the contractions and delay calving.

At the end of the preparatory stage the cervix expands, allowing the uterus and vagina to become a continuous canal. A portion of the placenta (water sac) is forced into the pelvis and aids in the dilation of the cervix. This water sac usually ruptures and the membranes hang from the vulva until Stage 2.

Stage 2

Delivery (1 to 2 hours, may be longer in heifer). This stage begins when the fetus enters the birth canal and usually occurs while the cow is lying down. Uterine contractions are now about every 2 minutes and are accompanied by voluntary contractions of the diaphragm and abdominal muscles.

Surrounded by membranes, the calf's forelegs and nose now protrude from the vulva. After the nose is exposed, the dam exerts maximum straining to push the shoulders and chest through the pelvic girdle. Once the shoulders have passed, the abdominal muscles of the calf relax and its hips and hind legs extend back to permit easier passage of the hip region.

The calf is normally born free of fetal membranes (placenta), because they remain attached to the cotyledons or "buttons" of the uterus. This ensures an oxygen supply for the calf during birth. Upon passage through the vulva, the umbilical cord generally breaks, respiration begins, filling the lungs with air and causing the lungs to become functional.

Delivery normally is completed in one hour or less in mature cows. Special assistance is warranted if this stage goes beyond 2 to 3 hours. First-calf heifers can take 1 to 2 hours, or longer. Proper judgment should be used so that assistance is neither too hasty, nor too slow.

Stage 3

Cleaning (2 to 8 hours). The caruncleo cotyledon, or button attachment between the uterus and placenta, relaxes and separates after parturition. The placenta is then expelled by continued uterine contractions. Cows normally expel the placenta within 2 to 8 hours.

Help Calf Start Breathing In Beef Cattle Calving Assistance

Occasionally you may find you need to help calf start breathing, these brief instructions will help.

Once delivered, clear any mucus from the calf's mouth and throat with your hand. Then, if necessary, stimulate the calf to breathe by either rubbing it briskly, tickling the inside of the nostril with a straw or slapping it with the flat of the hand.

Artificial respiration can be applied to the calf as follows: place a short section of garden hose into one nostril, hold mouth and nostrils shut so air enters and leaves only through the hose, then alternately blow into the hose and allow expiration of air. Repeat at 5- to 7-second intervals until the calf begins to breathe.

Another method is to alternate pressure and release on the rib cage.

Commercial respirators are also available and may be a wise investment in larger herds.

Beef Cattle Post Calving

Here are a few things to watch for as possible post calving problems.

Uterine prolapse

This is an inversion of the uterus that can occur when a partial vacuum is formed in the uterus. It is sometimes caused by pulling the calf too rapidly and may result in death of the cow if not treated promptly and correctly. Encouraging the cow to stand soon after delivery will reduce the chances of a prolapse.

Always contact a veterinarian for treatment and necessary drugs. Cull heifers or cows that prolapse because of the probability of it happening again.

Retained placenta

The placental membranes are normally expelled within 2 to 8 hours after birth. Occasionally, however, they fail to separate from the uterine attachment. This condition may pose a health threat to the cow and cause problems in rebreeding. Not all reasons for retained placentas are known, but high incidence may indicate a disease problem. They commonly accompany difficult births, multiple births and short gestations.

There are differing opinions as to the best treatment for retained placentas. Research has shown that manual removal can cause complications that would not have happened otherwise. For cows with no signs of abnormal vaginal discharges, good appetite and good milk production, no treatment may be best of all. If antibiotics are to be placed in the uterus, care must be taken to prevent introduction of bacteria through contaminated instruments or equipment. Boluses may reduce fertility of the cow. Antibiotics by injection or intrauterine application requires attention to residue avoidance in the sale of the milk or animal for food.

Beef Cattle Calving Assistance Summary

Here is a summary of the more important steps involved with your beef cattle calving assistance procedures.

1. Observe the herd closely during calving season, especially first-calf heifers because they will require the most assistance.

2. Have the proper equipment and facilities available prior to calving and in clean, working order.

3. Give assistance during delivery or call a veterinarian when needed. Do not wait more than a few hours after labor begins to act.

4. Correct any abnormal fetal positions in the early stages of delivery.

5. When pulling a calf, loop the chain or rope around the pastern. Apply gentle traction on one leg at a time to facilitate passage of the shoulders through the birth canal.

6. Remove mucus from the calf's nose and mouth immediately after birth. If the calf does not start to breathe normally, tickle the nostrils, hold it up by the hind legs and shake it, or apply artificial respiration with a piece of hose or by alternating pressure and release on the rib cage.

7. Disinfect the navel cord with iodine to prevent infection. Make sure the calf nurses within an hour after

birth or give colostrum to weak calves.

8. Keep birth weight and ease-of-calving records to identify those sires and dams responsible for calving problems. This information is especially important for selecting sires to breed yearling heifers. When possible, cull those females with a history of calving problems and avoid selecting replacement heifers from such cows.

You should always consult with your veterinarian for further information or assistance when in doubt.

Beef Cattle Health Care

Cattle Health Problems

Cattle of all ages, and especially young, growing cattle are subject to a variety of ailments. They range from mild conditions to severe infectious diseases that may cause death within 24 hours.

The cost of caring for sick cattle can seriously reduce your profit margin. With the increasing need to cut production costs, good herd health care is very important for any beef operation.

Prevention is the easiest and cheapest method of disease control. Clean sheds, lots, feed and water troughs give disease less chance to get started. A sound vaccination program, parasite control, and frequent observation of the herd also help to reduce the occurrence of illness.

You can recognize a sick animal first by its abnormal behavior or physical appearance. Droopy ears, loss of appetite, head down, scouring (diarrhea), or inactivity may indicate illness. A high temperature usually indicates disease.

The best course of action is to find a sick animal quickly, treat it, and then work to eliminate the cause of the sickness. If one or two animals come down with a disease, the rest of the herd has been or will be exposed to it.

Health problems are more common during and after periods of stress, including calving, weaning, shipping, working or moving the cattle, and extreme weather conditions. Stress can reduce an animal's ability to resist infectious agents. After a period of stress, give extra attention to your animals' health.

Some Common cattle problems
Respiratory diseases

Respiratory diseases are common in cattle. A number of factors contribute to an outbreak: inadequate nutrition, stress, and viral or bacterial infection. Good management and vaccination of cows and calves is the best way to prevent outbreaks of respiratory disease. Your veterinarian or Extension agent can help you develop a program to reduce losses on your ranch and in the feedlot.

White muscle disease

White muscle disease is a serious problem in many areas, check with your veterinarian for your area. It is caused by a dietary deficiency of the trace mineral selenium. It may cause paralysis of the skeletal muscles or may affect the heart muscle, causing respiratory distress and death within a few hours.

If you are in an area where white muscle disease is likely to occur, supply adequate amounts of selenium in the diet. In addition, injecting newborn calves with a commercial selenium/vitamin E preparation is a short term solution. Your veterinarian can advise you regarding the incidence of disease in your area.

Brucellosis (Bang's disease)

Brucellosis is a serious disease. It causes abortion and sterility in cattle, bison, elk, and deer, and undulant fever in humans.

Federal and state laws effectively outline brucellosis control. Vaccination is recommended for all heifers before they are 12 months old.

Brucellosis most commonly enters a herd through the purchase of infected cattle. To help prevent brucellosis from entering your herd, vaccinate all heifers between ages 4 to 10 months, and purchase only brucellosis-vaccinated cattle.

External Parasites

External parasites include horn flies, face flies, stable flies, heel flies, and lice. The largest health problem comes from the additional stress these insects cause to animals. When infested, cattle spend more time in the shade and don't graze, which causes poor performance.

You can reduce these problems by using fly-repellent ear tags or another parasite control treatment. Eliminating the areas where pests reproduce also helps to reduce the severity of external parasites.

Internal parasites

Internal parasites such as roundworms, lungworms, and liver flukes commonly occur in cattle. These hidden parasites cause poor performance and occasionally kill young animals.

Cattle are likely to pick up internal parasites when they graze established pastures. Internal parasites also can be a problem in confined areas.

Invasion of the stomach or intestinal wall by a parasite leads to poor digestion of nutrients and damage to organs. Signs of parasite infestation include scouring, rough hair coat, poor gains, and potbelly appearance.

Use dewormers at strategic times during the year to reduce the number of internal parasites. Use fecal sampling to determine the severity of the infestation and the type of dewormer that will be effective.

Bloat

Bloat may cause sudden death of an affected animal. Avoid grazing cattle on lush alfalfa. Other plants may also cause problems for cattle so it would be wise to have your County Agent or veterinarian visit your pasture and corral area and determine any potential plant problems that may be present. It is important that any supplemental feeds used be free of mold and spoilage. Avoid sudden feed changes; make gradual changes over 10 to 14 days, especially when adding grain to the ration. Bloat may be considered a disease which can affect animals in confinement fed mixtures of alfalfa and concentrate. Symptoms are similar as well as treatment which should be discussed with a veterinarian.

Scours or Diarrhea

Scours or diarrhea is common in newborn calves and animals of a young age. Cows must receive adequate protein and energy during pregnancy, especially the last 60 days to provide immunity to disease for the newborn. The newborn calf must also receive colostrums, the cow's first milk, within 1 to 6 hours of birth in order to develop immunity or antibodies against disease. A clean environment is also essential for the cow just prior to and after calving. The basic treatment for scours is fluid and electrolytes to maintain hydration of the calf.

Clostridial Diseases

A group of related diseases may cause sudden death, especially in young, growing cattle. These diseases are Blackleg, Enterotoxaemia, etc. Good vaccines are available and cattle should be vaccinated early in life with boosters at appropriate times. Your veterinarian can help you select the proper vaccine and outline a time schedule. This would include a 7-way Clostridial vaccine at 2 to 3 months of age and a second booster at weaning.

General

Injections of any type may cause lesions if injected into the muscles. All injections should be given subcutaneously (under the skin) when possible. Muscles in the neck can be used if it is necessary that intramuscular injections be given. DO NOT make injections into the hind quarters (rear legs or hip). Be sure to keep records of all treatments and always follow the withdrawal times as directed. The directions on the product will indicate how long the animal must be withheld from slaughter after use of the specific product. Always follow all directions on the label.

Disease Control

Vaccinations and parasite controls are available for many of the diseases affecting cattle. The choice of remedy and time of application depend on a variety of things, including the animal's nutritional level, disease prevalence in the herd, and the region in which the cattle are located. You should consult a veterinarian and Extension agent to develop a sound health program for your herd.

External Parasites In Beef Cattle

External parasites are a nuisance and a dangerous threat to cattle in any part of the world. These creatures can only live by feeding from the host animal and this ends up depleting the energy and nutrition stores of the host. When external parasites exist in a herd of beef cattle, there are many problems that result including:

• Weight loss

• Decreased meat and milk production

• Generalized weaknesses

• Skin problems like mange and dermatitis

• Potential secondary infections through skin wounds

• Transmission of diseases from ill animals to healthy stock

External parasites that affect beef cattle include

• Lice

• Flies

• Ticks

• Cattle Grubs

• Mites

Although the warmer months present the biggest problem for owners of beef cattle these external parasites are a year round problem that must be dealt with properly.

Beef Cattle and Flies

Flies are a common insect that has one set of wings and there are almost two dozen types of flies that affect beef cattle and other livestock. The main challenge that is presented with flies is that they do not live on the animals and only have sporadic contact with a herd.

Blood Sucking Flies

• Blood Sucking Flies include the black flies that are small insects with a humped back and a sturdy body. These external parasites are seen around the mucous membranes of the cattle including the eyes, ears, nose, and mouth. The females are the feeders and they will draw blood during the daytime. The bites of these insects are extremely irritating and can leave open sores. There have been animals that have died from anemia and allergic reactions to the bite of black flies. These blood sucking parasites lay eggs on fallen logs, branches, stones or other surfaces that are accessible in small eddies of streams.

• Horn Flies are another bloodsucker that can be troublesome to any beef cattle herd. These flies are aggressive biters and they can quickly create festering, open sores on the underline or head of an animal. Horn flies cluster when the bite and they show a preference to attack the withers and back of cattle. These parasites can transmit many diseases within a herd, especially anaplasmosis. If the number of Horn Flies per herd animal is 50 or greater, it is a threat and should be addressed, but some numbers greater that 20,000 per animal have been documented. This parasite lays eggs in extremely fresh manure that is less than 10 minutes old and the larvae hatch in less than 24 hours. The average female Horn fly can lay about 200 eggs during her life and 10-14 days is all that is needed for these insects to go from egg to adult. Horn Flies stay on their host animals continually and feed up to 20 times during a 24-hour period.

• Horse and Deer Flies are strong flying insects that also feed during the daytime and they have a notably vicious bite. These parasitic insects are responsible for much of the low weight gains and decreased milk production among many beef cattle operations. The frequency and severity of the bites of these two types of flies will often cause cattle to run or exhibit wild behavior. There are some herds that have been known to stampede due to attacks by Horse or Deer Flies. These two insects are known as Tabanids and they have an anticoagulant that is released into the host when they make the bite. This makes the animal ooze blood, which exposes them to bacterial diseases and other parasitic infections. Some of the diseases that can be transmitted by these insects include tularemia, anaplasmosis, and even anthrax. The eggs of these flies are laid in areas of vegetation and in other moist environments. Horse and Deer Flies have varying life spans depending on the particular species, but some can live as long as 2 years.

• Sand Flies are another blood-sucking parasite that affects beef cattle, particularly in the southern states. In the Southeast, they are frequently called "No See Ums". These creatures are more nuisance and aggravation than serious threat, but they can cause suffocation if their numbers are large enough. A few species of Sand Flies are also known to spread   nvolved s and blue tongue virus among cattle herds.

• The Dog Fly (or Stable Fly) looks much like a house fly but it has a pronounced mouth made for biting and both males and females will feast on livestock if they are not controlled. The bites from these external parasites causes discomfort and blood loss. They are known to transmit both anaplasmosis and anthrax. Females can lay up to 600 eggs during their lifetime and these insects mature in as little as 2 weeks. Their total life span is 21 to 58 days. If there are more than 10 of these flies per animal in a herd of cattle it can be crippling economically.

Non-Blood Sucking External Parasites

• Cattle Grubs consist of two species in the US. There is the common cattle grub as well as the Northern variety. At present, the common cattle grub is found only in the state of Florida and the Northern cattle grub appears on those beef cattle living in other states. The common cattle grub lays eggs mostly on the hair of the animals and can attach up to 15 eggs on just one hair. The eggs will hatch in 3-4 days and then the maggots will tunnel into the skin of the animal. The common cattle grub larvae will move to the mucous membranes of the gullet while the Northern variety will move into the spinal cord. During the fall months, these larvae will move to the back of their host cattle and will eat a hole through to the outside so that they can breathe. When the larva is ready to pupate, each will push through the skin and drop to the ground. Because of these larvae, the animal experiences great discomfort and irritation. It suffers from fatigue and decreases in weight gain and milk production. The open sores can also lead to infection and other illnesses. The animal carcass will also show the infestation and any meat near the grubs will be foul and discolored leading to waste. Even the hide value is decreased greatly because of the holes found in the animal skin.

• When Fly Maggots are present in the host animal's tissue it is known as Myiasis. One of the most notorious of all the maggots is the Primary Screwworm. This parasite only feeds on live tissue. The Southeast have been able to eradicate the problem, but there is always a chance for it to return.

• Secondary Screwworms and Blow Flies also feed on the sores of animals and can infest any open wounds.

Lice

Lice are parasitic throughout their life stages. They are very species specific and lice that may affect horses will not bother cattle, and vice versa. Some of the louse species will only suck nourishment from their host animal, but there is a cattle biting louse that creates skin irritations and discomfort year round. Fall to early spring are the times when lice population explodes and during the summer they tend to be a minimal problem for beef cattle herds. Lice are transferred by contact and can cause animals to be nervous and irritable. Many lice infected cattle will show weight loss, listlessness, and raw areas on their hide.

Mites

Mites have short life spans from 8 days to a month and most are barely able to be seen without the aid of a microscope. One of these parasitic species is the Mange Mites that tunnel just under the hide of a host animal. The tunnels will have dried, scabby nodules at the opening and the cattle will constantly rub and scratch trying to relieve the discomfort. An infested host can develop wide spread infection and large scabs over the body. It is imperative that all animals in the herd be treated to halt the attack from these contagious parasites.

Mosquitoes and Ticks

Mosquitoes and ticks are small insects but they can create a great deal of discomfort and pain in a cattle herd. Both of these parasitic insects can be the reason for weight loss, decreased milk production, and anemia in beef cattle. The bites from these animals also spread many diseases, and the bites can create sores that lead to secondary infections.

Conclusion

With the many different types of external parasites that threaten beef cattle herds it is important to be alert to any danger. Taking measures to prevent external parasites is the first step to a healthy herd. Even the most stringent prevention can still fail to keep all of the parasitic threats at bay. Identifying the problem early and handling the treatment quickly and appropriately is necessary for optimum cattle safety and health.

Controlling External Parasites In Beef Cattle

In order for anyone to maintain the comprehensive health of a herd of beef cattle it is necessary to plan and follow a systematic program of external parasite control. Each year the US cattle industry loses hundreds of millions of dollars because of the destructive effects of parasites. Flies, ticks, mites, grubs and lice are all part of this national problem.

Cattle owners lose money in many different ways but primarily parasites create loss through
• Reduction of animal performance
• Decreased milk production and ability
• Decreased fertility
• Loss of market value

External Parasites- Control Program for Beef Cattle

External parasites of beef cattle can be controlled by using a wide variety of products:
• ear tags
• sprays
• Wet applications or pour-on insecticides

- Dusts
- back rubbers
- Mineral additives

Ear tags that contain organophosphate or man made pyrethroids are easy ways to use insecticides that can control flies and ticks. These have been used for almost 30 years but some cattle owners have had varying results due to misuse. When ear tags were first used the flies would be off the animal in 15 minutes. However these ear tags have been overused and this has led to resistance among the fly population on many of the farms. Here are the proper directions that should be used with ear tags or "fly tags".

- Use two tags, one in each ear for every animal

- Tag the calves

- Use the ear tags beginning around the 15th of May, if they are used too early the medication will run out before fly season is over

- Remove the ear tags in the fall around October 1st

• Rotate the types of ear tags you use every year so you do not use the same insecticide compounds continually. If you are using ear tags with an organophosphate compound this year you should switch to tags with a man-made pyrethroid compound next year.

External Parasite Application Treatments

Some people will choose specific parasite treatments that need to be applied to the animal's body. These can be very effective but must be used correctly.

• Only apply these medications or insecticides on a day when rain is not forecast. If it rains during the first 4 hours after you applied the treatment then the water will render it useless.

• Sprays and pour on applications for external parasites can be used but directions must be followed carefully and contamination of food and water should be avoided. Always use a glove, safety goggles and mask when applying any dust or liquid medication to animals.

• Backrubbers and facerubbers can be used for control of lice and most of the biting insects. These must be kept charged and daily use will provide the best results. Only use#2 diesel grade oil or approved backrubber base oil.

• Dust bags can be used with good results but must be hung where cows will come in contact with them. Protect the dust bags from rainy weather to prolong their use. If you choose a hand dusting method for applying insecticides to cattle you need to make sure that you contact the skin under the hair.

Important Reminders Regarding External Parasite Treatment and Control for Cattle

• Sprays for Grub control should only be used between August 1 and November 1. If used after this time the larva can be in vital areas of the cow's system and the spray can result in bloat, paralysis or death of the animal.

• Fly control should be started in mid-March or no later than mid-April.

• I know of no internal or external parasite treatment that lasts for 6 months.

• Internal and external parasite treatments for beef cattle will be effective for 1-2 months only.

• Treat cattle for grub and lice in the early fall and again in January or in February.

• Check with your veterinarian to determine the best parasite control system to use for the needs of your herd.

Internal Parasites In Beef Cattle

Beef cattle are at risk for internal parasites and this is particularly true for animals that graze in pastures. The parasitic levels vary for every pasture however, and are dependent on the species of cattle. These are some documented facts regarding internal parasites and beef cattle.

• If a pasture is heavily stocked the risk of internal parasitic involvement is increased.

• Beef cattle from a dry lot show fewer infestations of internal parasites than those animals kept in pastures.

• Young cattle are known to present with more internal parasites than their older counterparts.

Cattle farmers and herd owners should understand what problems are caused by internal parasites and be familiar with the most common types.

Effects of Internal Parasites on Beef Cattle

The effects of any internal parasites will depend on the degree of infection, and the age and condition of the affected animal. Cattle that develop parasitic infections can show one or more of the following problems:

- Decreased productivity of milk
- Lack of weight gain
- Rough coat
- Anemia
- Edema
- Diarrhea
- Spontaneous abortions or infertility problems
- Decreased energy
- Listless behavior

Animals with Greatest Risk of Internal Parasite Infection

The most likely cattle to be infected with one or more internal parasites are
- Bulls
- Animals that are under stress, especially during early lactation
- Cattle that are very young

Most mature bovines will have developed a level of immunity to most of these internal parasitic threats.

Internal Parasites that are a Threat to Cattle

Beef cattle can fall victim to a number of internal attackers including Helminths and Protozoans. The most common threat is from the Helminths or "worms".

• roundworms (or nematodes)

• tapeworms (or cestodes)

• flukes or (trematodes)

Economic Threat is Greatest with Roundworms

The Roundworms are one of the most crushing threats economically to the livestock owners in many states. There are 2 common roundworms that create the most problems;

• the brown stomach worm

• Cooperia

Although the tapeworms and flukes can be a problem with some herds they do not present as much of an economic threat because the effect on the cattle is less. Flukes are only a problem if the snail population is allowed to expand because these worms need the snail to complete their life cycle.

Conclusion

It is obvious that an internal parasite can be a big concern with any beef cattle herd. The roundworms have a life cycle that makes it possible for one or two infected animals to spread the worms to the entire herd. Internal infestations are often difficult to notice in the early stages which means by the time the problem is recognized other animals will have been exposed and possibly infected. Understanding the causes, knowing the effects created by internal worms, and taking preventive measures for your animals will decrease your chance of having to deal with these potentially devastating parasites. If internal parasites should occur within your beef cattle herd there are some specific ways that you can handle the problem so that you can minimize your losses.

Controlling Internal Parasites in Beef Cattle

Internal parasites live in the digestive tract and lungs of cattle throughout the world. These internal parasites can result in a very significant economic loss to anyone engaged in beef cattle operations. Protozoans and worms compete with the animal for the available nutrients and this reduces the animal's production, weight gain and milk production. Cattle that are infected with internal parasites are also at great risk for anemia and other health problems.

Although parasites are often treated in the fall it is more cost effective and beneficial to treat the animals in both the spring and the fall. This will reduce the risk of passing the parasites on through waste elimination in the pasture. Treating the cattle twice a year will also make the pasture a safer area for calves at grazing time.

Parasites that exist internally in cattle have different life cycles. Some of these worms develop inside the animal and others have a life cycle that must take place in the cattle's manure. When the infected manure contaminates food or water sources for the cows the parasites can then spread rapidly. Even the cold of winter may not kill the larva and eggs that are in the manure. The parasites will often remain dormant until the next grazing season.

The best way to achieve internal parasite control is to eradicate as many of the parasites as possible from all of the infected animals. This will help minimize the risk of parasite infection to calves and other herd members that are parasite free. There are several ways for a beef cattle owner to manage and control internal parasites.

Lower Stocking Rates

If your herd has high stocking rates it makes it difficult to control and eliminate internal parasites. Too many cattle grazing on the same land area means that some are forced to use forage that has been contaminated. Lower stocking rates in a pasture will decrease the spread of infection and reduce the amount of parasites that come in contact with the animals.

Rotate Pasture Lands

When a pasture is allowed to rest it gives nature a chance to clean and refresh the land. Parasitic eggs and larvae can be killed when exposed to long periods of uninterrupted sun, rain and fresh air. Without the requisite host animals the life cycle is interrupted and often terminated.

Clean Water

Utilizing watering systems designed for pastures will give a cattle herd fresh, clean water that is free from parasitic contamination.

Using Anthelmintics

If internal parasites are a pressing concern it may be necessary to treat not only the infected animals, but the entire herd as well.Beef cattle dewormers come in different forms including pour on formulas, boluses, feed and mineral additives, pastes, drenches and injectables. There are two basic classes of products that are used to rid cattle of worms.

• Fenbendazole and Levamisole

• Avermectins (abamectin, doramectin, moxidectin, ivermectin)

Fenbendazole and Levamisole will kill adult parasites and any larvae that may be present when the treatment is given. The chemicals are quickly eliminated by the cattle and do not interfere with a future slaughter date. Some parasites can be left alive if they are in a life cycle stage that the chemicals do not effect. This is why a repeat treatment application must be given within 2-4 weeks from the initial dose.

Avermectins also destroy parasites in the cattle but these chemicals remain in the body for a much longer period and remain effective during this time. These preparations can kill the parasites more effectively and do not require frequent administration. Avermectins are more effective at parasite control but they are also more expensive to buy and use.

When to Treat Cattle for Grubs

Cattle owners can use avermectin class antiparisiticals as a pour on to effectively control all stages of cattle grubs. Grubs are classified as both an internal and external cattle parasite and they can be tricky to treat. If the animals are treated when the larvae is in the tissues of the esophagus it can create bloat. If the cattle are treated when the grub larvae are in the spinal canal the animals can stagger or become paralyzed. In both cases the animals have a high risk of death. Any cattle treatment for grubs must be done when the larvae are not in vital tissue areas. A veterinarian can help you plan your internal parasite control program.

New Beef Cattle Farming Enterprise and the Farm Location

Farm Location is extremely important for a successful Small beef cattle farming or ranching operation. You should select your farm location wisely.

Is the enterprise compatible with the community?

Is the property zoned for large animal production?

How many animals can you have?

How will neighbors react to the project?

Land:

Your land resource is of utmost importance. Some acreage may or may not be suitable for pasture production.

Is irrigation water available?

When is the water available?

What kind of an irrigation system is in place?

You may need to contact a local irrigation company to find answers to some of these questions.

A corral or dry lot must be available to keep the animals in when irrigating or when the pasture needs a rest.

Corrals are also essential if finishing cattle on grain rations.

If there is adequate acreage you may consider farming and raising some of your own feed. Realize that it is expensive to own and maintain equipment. It may not be economically feasible to own equipment, although custom operators are sometimes an option.

Forage Production and Carrying Capacity:

There are several factors that affect forage production: season, rainfall, availability of irrigation water, soil conditions, soil fertility, plant varieties, and grazing management.

Pastures are normally grazed from early spring into late fall or usually only about half the year. During some years grazing may be available for a longer or shorter period and must be planned for. In most areas the greatest forage production and quality for grass pastures usually occurs from May 15 until July 15.

Cattle performance and carrying capacity are related to and affected by forage production and quality. Carrying capacity and cattle performance are not simple to predict and will change from month to month. For example, during the month of June you may be able to graze five, 500 pound calves per acre and have them gain two pounds per head per day. However, during the month of August you may only be able to graze three, 500 pound calves per acre and have them gain one pound per head per day. This presents a challenge to your pasture management but must be planned for if you are to be successful.

The Human Resource:

You and your family may gain a lot of satisfaction from raising a few cattle. Children can benefit from the added responsibility and families can be strengthened as they work together. However, the project will require a commitment of time. Even when cattle are on pasture they need to be observed daily to make sure that they have adequate feed and water and to assure that they are healthy.

Facilities:

In the production of cattle on small acreages it is not necessary to provide more than the basic facilities. Some necessary facilities would be a means of constraint such as a head gate and alley way, trough or feeder for supplemental feeds, and proper fencing. There must also be available a clean and continual source of water to the animal.

Humane care of animals is legislated and must be adhered to so provide facilities that will accommodate animal welfare. These would include care for the animal in all aspects of its life, such as proper feed, handling facilities, shelter and the removal of any or all conditions which may inflict stress on the animal. If unsure of any of these principles consult with your local Extension Agent or Veterinarian.

When cattle need to be treated or handled it is necessary to restrain them for their safety and the safety of the people handling them. Commercially manufactured squeeze chutes offer excellent restraint, however, they are expensive. Plans are available from the Extension Service for building homemade chutes constructed of metal or lumber. These are generally adequate when handling a small number of cattle.

Good fences are important to insure safety and good relationships with neighbors. Electric fences are useful for pasture management, and perimeter fences should be sufficiently strong, high and tight to contain the animals. A four and a half foot fence made of woven wire, six strands of barbed wire or a combination of the two is adequate. Corral fences should be at least five feet high and constructed of wood or metal. Woven wire and barbed wire are not recommended in areas where cattle are being crowded or handled.

Troughs are necessary if cattle are being fed grain. A feed bunk or commercially available feeder is necessary to minimize waste when cattle are fed hay in a confined area.

Cattle do well in the cold of winter if they have a wind break and a dry place to bed down. Corrals tend to get wet and muddy in the winter and spring. Cattle either need some high dry ground or a shelter.

Essay - Raising Beef Cattle For Profit Today

Interesting reading; see if you can relate to it?

This was the result of asking in a public forum for an essay related to "Raising Beef Cattle For Profit Today". But, Please if you are an experienced cattleman remember that today there is only 2% or less of the population   nvolved in Agriculture. Have you ever heard it said that 2% feed the other 98%?

Back To The Essay

Raising Beef Cattle is much different than raising dairy cattle. The beef cows, or feeder cattle as it is called, are much larger. Although the primary reason for Raising Beef Cattle for Profit on a Small Farm is for their meat production; however, there are many other things that cattle are used for. There is not much that is not used from cattle when they are sold to meat companies. The cattle are very carefully slaughtered, and great care is taken when they are skinned; the hides are used in all sorts of leather products, and the insides are used in shampoos and cosmetics. This beef meat is cut into steaks, ribs, roasts, and ground beef.

The list of Beef Cattle is very long and some types are more popular than others, such as the Black Angus, the Brahman, the Hereford, and the Long Horn. Many countries have produced their own breeds of Beef Cattle. Great Britain and Ireland developed the White Park, which is a very hardy beef cow.

The Texas Longhorn from Texas USA is a great beef steer to Raise Beef Cattle for Profit on a Small Farm. The horns can reach 120 inches in length, and they are very hardy in dry climates.

The Murray Grey, which comes from Eastern Australia, is a breed from a Shorthorn cow and an Angus bull, and they are very easy to take care of. They are so popular that many have been shipped to other countries for breeding.

The Nelore is a breed from India, and has been exported to Brazil where it has become the most dominate breed in that area.

The Longhorns from the Midlands of England have very long horns that curve, forming a circle. They are of medium size and are very hardy.

The Australian Braford, a breed that was a cross between Herefords and Brahmans, has a high resistance from ticks as well as from the daytime heat.

These are just a few of the great types of beef cattle that can be raised. However, there are still some very important things that need to be considered when it comes to Raising Beef Cattle for Profit on a Small Farm.

You need to feed beef cattle the proper amounts to food, with the best nutrition as possible; a fat steer is how you earn your money. You also need to keep plenty of clean clear water for them.

Pasture for grazing is another very important item for Raising Beef Cattle for Profit on a Small Farm. Although some small farms may not have as much pasture room as larger ranches, or larger cattle farms, you can get around this by giving your cattle some good grades of hey when the grazing is not up to par, such as in the winter time.

If you want to begin Raising Beef Cattle for Profit on a Small Farm, and you do not fully understand what to do. There lots of books that have been written that can help you. Some of these books can give you great advice and show pictures of just how something should look. The books are written by expert cattlemen that want to help the new guy. You can search the internet also to find all sorts of information about Raising Beef Cattle for Profit on a Small Farm.

Do You Really Want To Be A Farm Mom

Remembering a Day In The Life Of Most Farm Mothers in the 1930's.

Farm Life was good, though each day was a little long because it was always before light and until after dark!

Mom was up a couple hours before first light every morning. Light the kerosene lamp to light the kitchen enough to search for something to fix for breakfast. No easy task because farm life in those days required a huge family breakfast. At our house the main fare was usually home made biscuits, hen eggs, milk gravy, fried potatoes and depending on the time of year maybe a side helping of pork, bacon, ham or sausage. Top that off with some kind of home canned jelly, home raised honey or home cooked molasses.

Thirty minutes before mom had breakfast finished it is time to wake the rest of the house.

Dad has to hurry and get his clothes and other stuff

ready for a 3 mile walk to work; he worked on the railroad, manual labor (was there any other kind in those days). Mom had made him and the school age kids a sack lunch from some of the breakfast food she had just cooked. (Have you ever had a biscuit and fried potato sandwich?).

Family breakfast is now on the table and kids are dragged in. It was a requirement that the entire family had to be at the table when each meal started and remain there until everyone was finished. Once to the table it never took much coaxing to get everyone to eat a hearty breakfast because they knew it was the main meal until supper time which was usually about dark.

Breakfast is over, dad is off to work and mom is washing the dishes by hand while waiting for the first light of day. That little chore needs to be finished by the breaking of first light. More to do outside when it is light enough to see.

Time to milk the cows and take care of the other livestock. This little job required taking the kids along so she could teach them to milk the cows, slop the hogs and take care of all the farm critters. Taking care of the livestock was done before milking because once the milking is over it was necessary to get the milk to the house to prevent getting dirt in the open top milk bucket. Most all farms had a milking stool and ours was no different, however our stool also doubled as a feed bucket.

That little chore is done and the kids only got squirted with milk once this morning. Now back to the house, strain the milk, set the container of milk in cool water to keep it fresh. Sometimes excess milk was set aside to allow the cream to rise to the top for skimming to make butter. Hot biscuits were a lot better if you had butter, still the same today.

Sometimes there were more cows and they produced more milk than the family could use. When this happened there was a hand crank separator to collect the cream and it was saved in five or ten gallon milk and placed out by the road in a tub of water. It was picked up by milk route man and taken to a creamery for making butter and cheese. It paid a little bit and helped buy a few staples. The skim milk was fed back to the chickens and pigs.

Now it's time to get the school age kids off to school. Be

sure each one has their lunch and books if any were brought home the previous day (bringing school books home was a rarity and privilege).

Kids are off to school. Is it time to rest? Did Farm Life allow mother's any time for R&R? Not in this case. It was now time to work the vegetable garden and after that the cotton and corn fields. Kids not old enough for school were taken along to the fields. What fun! This was somewhat relaxing though because there were less people responsibilities with dad off to work on the railroad and the older kids off to school. Didn't last long though because kids started getting home from school about 4:30 pm (Does this sound a little late? They walked to and from school).

Kids are home now and looking for a snack but very seldom being treated to one, sorry you will have to wait until supper time. You can go out to play a few minutes before we do the regular chores. Same routine as in the morning with one added chore of gathering the hen eggs.

After chores, time to start supper, not too surprising many of the supper time meals consisted of the same menu as breakfast. Most all of the food had been raised on the farm. It was good though because the menu would change based on the season of the year. In spring and summer maybe a few fresh vegetables from the garden and in the fall it would be canned stuff or maybe dried beans and peas.

Even with breakfast and supper menu being the same, they were big meals and occasionally the meat might change from pork to chicken. Now for Sunday when company comes add fresh vegetables and those pies mom made earlier, and everyone has an exceptionally big meal.

In spite of the tough schedule everyone loved being there and never complained. After all Farm Life was and still is the good life. Now can you imagine how many of today's modern city folk can survive a good farm life like that and do it without complaining.

Glossary Of Terms Related To The Beef Cattle Industry

 Accuracy (of selection)--Correlation between an animal's unknown actual breeding value and a calculated estimated breeding value.

Adaptation -- Adaptation to a particular environment exists when an animal or breed has the ability to survive, produce and reproduce within that environment at an acceptable level to the cattle producer.

Adaptive Trait -- An adaptive trait is one that contributes to an animal or a breed's ability to survive and reproduce sustainably in a particular environment. Resistance to internal parasites and heat tolerance are important adaptive traits in some environments but not in others.

Average daily gain (ADG)--Measurement of daily body weight change in animal on a feed test. Most bull tests are 140 or 160 days in length.

Adjusted weaning weight (WW)--An unshrunk, off-the-cow weight adjusted to 205 days of age and to a mature dam age equivalence.

Adjusted yearling weight (YW)--An unshrunk weight adjusted to either 365, 452, or 550 days of age and for age of dam.

Ad lib feeding--No limit placed on amount of feed intake. Self-feeding or allowing cattle to consume feed on a free-choice basis.

Allele -- Alleles at a gene locus have different nucleotide sequences within the DNA. Because different alleles may have different biological effects, they account for the genetic variation necessary for response to selection. See also gene. Alleles may also described as alternate forms of genes. Because genes occur in pairs in body cells, one gene of a pair may have one effect and another gene of that same pair (allele) may have a different effect on the same trait.

Artificial insemination (A.I.)--The technique of placing semen from the male in the reproductive tract of the female by means other than natural service. ~

Backcross--The mating of a two-breed crossbred offspring

back to one of its parental breeds. Example: A Hereford-Angus cross cow bred back to an Angus bull.

Beef carcass data service--A program whereby producers, for a fee, can receive carcass evaluation data on their cattle by using a special "carcass data" eartag for their slaughter animals. See county extension director breed representative, Beef Cattle Improvement Association representative, or area office of USDA meat grading service for information.

Beef Improvement Federation (BIF)--A federation of organizations, businesses, and individuals interested or involved in performance evaluation of beef cattle. The purposes of BIF are to bring about uniformity of procedures, development of programs, cooperation among interested entities, education of its members and the ultimate consumers of performance evaluation methods, and to build confidence of the beef industry in the principles and potentials of performance testing.

Birth weight (BW)--The weight of a calf taken within 24 hours after birth. Heavy birth weights tend to be correlated with calving problems, but the conformation of the calf and the cow are contributing factors.

Breeder--In most beef breed associations, the owner of the dam of a calf at the time she was mated or bred to produce that calf.

Breeding Objective -- The precise goal of a beef cattle breeding program is known as its breeding objective. An example would be "to produce high-quality, lean beef at the lowest possible cost." The breeding objective typically includes a listing of production and indicator traits that will be used as selection criteria. Breeding objectives vary among enterprises because of differences in resources, environments, markets and economic goals.

Breeding program goals--The objective or "direction" of breeder's selection programs. Goals are basic decisions breeders must make to give "direction" to their breeding program. Goals should vary among breeders due to relative genetic merit of their cattle, their resources, and their markets.

Breeding Value -- An animal's breeding value reflects its transmissible genetic merit for a trait. It is twice the amount by which progeny of the individual would differ from progeny of an average individual from the same population when mates of both were chosen at random from the population at large. Breeding value cannot be known with certainty, but it can be estimated using performance information from the animal itself and from its relatives. Directional selection is often practiced using expected progeny difference or EPD (one-half of estimated breeding value) as the selection criterion. Breeding value of an animal as a parent. The working definition is twice the difference between a very large number of progeny and the population average when individuals are mated at random within the population and all progeny are managed alike. The difference is doubled because only a sample half (one gene of each pair) is transmitted from a parent to each progeny. Breeding value exists for each trait and is dependent on the population in which the animal is evaluated. For a given trait, an individual can be an above average producer in one herd and a below average producer in another herd.

British breeds--Breeds of cattle such as Angus, Hereford, and Shorthorn originating in Great Britain.

Calf crop--The number or percentage of calves produced within a herd in a given year relative to the number of cows and heifers exposed to breeding.

Calving difficulty (Dystocia)--Abnormal or difficult labor, causing difficulty in delivering the fetus and/or placenta.

Calving season--The season(s) of the year when the calves are born. Limiting calving seasons is the first step to performance testing the whole herd, accurate records, and consolidated management practices.

Carcass evaluation--Techniques of measuring components of quality and quantity in carcasses.

Carcass merit--Desirability of a carcass relative to quantity of components (muscle, fat, and bone), USDA quality grade, plus potential eating qualities.

Carcass quality grad--An estimate of palatability based primarily on marbling and maturity and generally to a lesser extent on color, texture, and firmness of lean. Days on feed and fat thickness (of 0.25 inches or more) are comparable to quality grade in estimating eating quality.

Carcass quantity--Amount of salable meat (muscle) the carcass will yield. Cutability is an estimate of this. (See its definition.)

Carrier--A heterozygous individual having one recessive gene and one dominant gene for a given pair of genes (alleles). For example, an animal with one gene for polledness and one gene for horns will be polled but can produce horned offspring when mated to another animal carrying the gene for horns

Central test--A location where animals are assembled from several herds to evaluate differences in certain performance traits under uniform management conditions.

Chromosome--Chromosomes are long DNA molecules on which genes (the basic genetic codes) are located. Domestic cattle have 30 pairs of chromosomes.

Closed herd--A herd in which no outside breeding stock (cattle) are introduced.

Collateral relatives--Relatives of an individual that are not its ancestors or descendants. Brothers and sisters are an example of collateral relatives.

Conception--The fertilization of the ovum (egg). The act of conceiving or becoming pregnant.

Congenital--Acquired during prenatal life. Condition exists at or dates from birth. Often used in the context of congenital (birth) defects.

Contemporary group--A group of cattle that are of the same breed and sex and have been raised in the same management group (same location on the same feed and pasture). Contemporary groups should include as many cattle as can be accurately compared.

Correlated Selection Response -- Correlated response to selection is the change that occurs in one or more traits as some other trait is subjected to directional selection. It occurs when some of the same genes affect the direct and correlated traits simultaneously, a phenomenon known as pleiotropy. Correlated responses may be beneficial, neutral or harmful, depending on the biology and economic impact of the traits in question. See also genetic correlation.

Correlation--A measure of how two traits vary together. A correlation of + 1.00 means that as one trait increases the other also increases a perfect positive relationship. A correlation of -1.00 means that as one trait increases the other decreases--a perfect negative, or inverse, relationship. A correlation of 0.00 means that as one trait increases, the other may increase or decrease--no consistent relationship. Correlation coefficients may vary between +1.00 and -1.00.

Crossbreeding--The mating of animals of different breeds (or species). Crossbreeding usually results in heterosis (hybrid vigor).

Culling--The process of eliminating less productive or less desirable cattle from a herd.

Cutability--An estimate of the percentage of salable meat (muscle) from a carcass versus percentage of waste fat. Percentage of retail yield of carcass weight can be estimated by a USDA prediction evaluation that includes hot carcass weight, ribeye area, fat thickness, and estimated percent of kidney, pelvic, and heart fat.

Dam--The female parent.

Decision-Support Programs -- A decision-support program is a set of rules, usually coded into a computer program, which allows a user to evaluate biological and economic impacts of breeding and management strategies on a production system.

Deviation-- difference between an individual record and the average for that trait for that contemporary group. These differences sum to zero when the correct average is used. A ratio deviation is the ratio less the average ratio or 100.

DNA Marker -- A DNA marker is a specific sequence on nucleotides within a particular gene that can be detected through laboratory analysis and can be used to determine which alleles are present at that locus in an individual. See also marker-assisted selection.

Dominance--Dominant genes affect the phenotype when present in either homozygous or heterozygous condition. A dominant gene need only be obtained from one parent to achieve expression.

Dystocia (calving difficulty)--Abnormal or difficult labor causing difficulty in delivering the fetus and/or placenta.

Economic value--The net return within a herd for making a pound or percentage change in the trait in question.

Effective progeny number (EPN)--An indication of the amount of information available for estimation of expected progeny differences in sire evaluation. It is a function of number of progeny but is adjusted for their distribution among herds and contemporary groups and for the number of contemporaries by other sires. EPN is less than the actual number because the distribution of progeny is never ideal.

Environment--All external (nongenetic) conditions that influence the reproduction, production, and carcass merit of cattle. In the context of beef cattle breeding, the environment includes the net effect of all nongenetic factors that influence an animal's phenotype for a particular trait, up until the time that the trait is observed or expressed. Factors that contribute to the environment include but are not limited to physical geography, climate, quantity and quality of the diet, management practices and health maintenance programs.

Embryo--A fertilized ovum (egg) in the earlier stages of prenatal development usually prior to development of body parts.

Embryo transfer--Removing fertilized ova (embryos) from one cow (donor dam) and placing these embryos into other cows (host cows), usually accompanied by hormone-induced superovulation of the donor dam. More calves can be obtained from cows of superior breeding value by this technique. Only proven producers should become donor dams.

Estimate--The process of calculating a particular value from data (verb). The value itself obtained from data (noun). The idea is that the true value is being obtained from the calculated value within limits of sampling variation.

Estimated breeding value (EBV)--An estimate of an individual's true breeding value for a trait based on the performance of the individual and close relatives for the trait. EBV is a systematic way of combining available performance information on the individual, brothers, and sisters of the individual, and the progeny of the individual.

Estrus (heat)--The recurrent, restricted period of sexual receptivity in cows and heifers. Nonpregnant cows and heifers usually come into heat 18 to 21 days following their previous estrus.

Expected progeny difference (EPD)--The difference in performance to be expected from future progeny of a sire, compared with that expected from future progeny of the average bull in the same test. EPD is an estimate based on progeny testing and is equal to one-half the estimate of breeding value obtainable from the progeny test records.

F1--Offspring resulting from the mating of a purebred (straightbred) bull to purebred (straightbred) females of another breed.

Feed conversion (feed efficiency)--Units of feed consumed per unit of weight gained. Also the production (meat, milk) per unit of feed consumed.

Frame score--A score based on subjective evaluation of

height or actual measurement of hip height. This score is related to slaughter weights at which cattle will grade choice or have comparable amounts of fat cover over the loin eye at the 12th to 13th rib.

Freemartin-- Female born twin to a bull calf (approximately 9 out of 10 will not conceive).

Generation interval--Average age of the parents when the offspring destined to replace them are born. A generation represents the average rate of turnover of a herd.

Gene -- A gene is a discrete segment of the DNA molecule, located at a specific site on a specific chromosome pair. The unique nucleotide sequence of each gene determines its specific biological function. Many genes specify the amino acid sequence of a protein product. Others produce molecules that are involved in controlling developmental and metabolic events. The basic units of heredity that occur in pairs and have their effect in pairs in the individual, but which are transmitted singly (one or the other gene at random of each pair) from each parent to offspring. See also allele.

Gene pool -- A population's gene pool is composed of all alleles at all gene loci on all chromosomes of individuals within that population. Its content is dependent upon the population's ancestry, historical isolation, history of natural and artificial selection and cumulative mutation.

Genetic Correlation -- The genetic correlation between two traits is a numerical measure of the extent to which variation in both of them is caused by genes at the same loci. It ranges from +1 (indicating that the two traits are genetically equivalent) through zero (indicating that the two traits are totally independent) to -1 (indicating that alleles causing the first trait to increase cause the other trait to decrease concomitantly). Correlations between two traits that arise because some of the same genes affect both traits. When two traits (i.e., weaning and yearling weight) are positively and highly correlated to one another successful selection for one trait will result in an increase in the other trait. When two traits are negatively and highly correlated (i.e., birth weight and calving ease) to one another, successful selection for one trait will result in a decrease in the other trait.

Genotype--Actual genetic makeup (constitution) of an

individual determined by its genes or germplasm. For example, there are two genotypes for the polled phenotype [PP (homozygous dominant) and Pp (heterozygote)].

Genotype By Environment Interaction -- Genotype by environment interaction exists when the difference in phenotypic merit between genetic groups is dependent upon the environment in which those groups are compared. Variation in the relative performance of different genotypes from one environment to another. For example, the "best" cattle (genotypes) for one environment may not be the "best" for another environment.

Gonad--The organ that produces the reproductive cells, the testicle in the male and the ovaries in the female.

Half-sibs--Individuals having the same sire or dam. Half-brothers and/or half-sisters.

Heat synchronization--Causing a group of cows or heifers to exhibit heat together at one time by artificial manipulation of the estrous cycle.

Heifer--A female of the cattle species less than three years of age that has not borne a calf.

Heredity--The transmission of genetic or physical traits of parents to their offspring.

Heritability -- Heritability is a numerical measure of the extent to which variation in a trait is genetically determined. Varying from zero to one, it describes the proportion of an individual's phenotypic superiority or inferiority for the trait expected to be transmitted to its offspring. The proportion of the differences among cattle, measured or observed, that is transmitted to the offspring. The higher the heritability of a trait, the more accurately does the individual performance predict breeding value and the more rapid should be the response due to selection for that trait.

Heritability estimate--An estimate of the proportion of the total phenotypic variation between individuals for a certain trait that is due to heredity. More specifically, hereditary variation due to additive gene action.

Heterosis -- Heterosis is the difference in average performance for a trait between crossbred individuals and the average performance of parent breeds contributing to the cross. It frequently is economically beneficial, particularly for traits that contribute to reproduction, longevity and health. Amount by which measured traits of the crossbreds exceed the average of the two or more purebreds that are mated to produce the crossbreds.

Heterozygous--Genes of a specific pair (alleles) are different in an individual.

Homozygous--Genes of a specific pair (alleles) are alike in an individual.

Inbreeding-Production of offspring from parents more closely related than the average of a population. Inbreeding increases the proportion of homozygous gene pairs and decreases the proportion of heterozygous gene pairs. Also, inbreeding increases prepotency and facilitates expression of undesirable recessive genes.

Inbreeding Coefficient -- The inbreeding coefficient is a number between zero and one that quantifies the expected reduction in proportion of heterozygous loci in the inbred individual, compared to the proportion of heterozygous loci in a typical individual from the noninbred population from which the individual descended.

Inbreeding Depression -- Inbreeding depression is the average change in phenotypic value for a trait that accompanies each unit of change in inbreeding coefficient within a population. Generally it is economically detrimental, particularly for traits that contribute to reproduction, longevity and health.

Independent culling levels--Selection of culling based on cattle meeting specific levels of performance for each trait included in the breeder's selection program. For example, a breeder could cull all heifers with weaning weights below 400 pounds (or those in the bottom 20 percent on weaning weight) and yearling weights below 650 pounds (or those in the bottom 40 percent).

Indicator Trait -- An indicator trait is one that does not directly influence net profit of commercial livestock production but which is genetically correlated with one or more traits that do. For example, larger scrotal circumference of yearling bulls does not increase revenue or reduce cost of production, but it is predictive of a bull's genetic merit for age at puberty, an economically important trait in many instances.

Involution--The return of an organ to its normal size or condition after enlargement, as of the uterus after parturition. A decline in size or activity of other tissues; the mammary gland tissues normally involute with advancing lactation.

Linebreeding--A form of inbreeding in which an attempt is made to concentrate the inheritance of some one ancestor, or line of ancestors, in a herd. The average relationship of the individuals in the herd to this ancestor (outstanding individual or individuals) is increased by linebreeding.

Linecross--Offspring produced by crossing two or more inbred lines.

Marbling--The specks of fat (intramuscular fat) distributed in muscular tissue. Marbling is usually evaluated in the ribeye between the 12th and 13th rib.

Marker-Assisted Selection -- In marker-assisted selection, DNA markers are used to predict genotypes of candidates for selection at loci associated with merit for an economically important trait. Such information may then be used in breeding value estimation for the trait.

Metabolic body size--The weight of the animal raised to the 3/4 power (W0.75); a figure indicative of metabolic needs and of the feed required to maintain a certain body weight.

Metabolism--The transformation by which energy is made available for body uses.

Most probable producing ability (MPPA)--An estimate of a cow's future productivity for a trait (such as progeny weaning weight ratio) based on her past productivity. For example, a cow's MPPA for weaning ratio is calculated from the cow's average progeny weaning ratio, the number of her progeny with weaning records, and the repeatability of weaning weight.

National sire evaluation--Programs of sire evaluation conducted by breed associations to compare sires on a progeny test basis. Carefully conducted national reference sire evaluation programs give unbiased estimates of expected progeny differences. Sire evaluations based on field data rely on large numbers of progeny per sire to compensate for possible favoritism or bias for sires within herds.

Nonadditive gene effects--Favorable effects or actions produced by specific gene pairs or combinations. Nonadditive gene action is the primary cause of heterosis. Nonadditive gene action occurs when the heterozygous genotype is not intermediate in phenotypic value to the two homozygous genotypes.

Number of contemporaries--The number of animals of similar breed, sex, and age, against which an animal was compared in performance tests. The greater the number of contemporaries, the greater the accuracy of comparisons.

Open--A term commonly used to indicate a non-pregnant female.

Optimum level of performance--The most profitable or favorable ranges in levels of performance for the economically important traits in a given environment and management system. For example, although many cows produce too little milk, in every management system there is a point beyond which higher levels of milk production may reduce fertility and decrease profit.

Outcrossing--Mating of individuals that are less closely related than the average of the breed. Commercial breeders and some purebred breeders should be outcrossing by periodically adding new sires that are unrelated to their cow herd. This outcrossing should reduce the possibility of loss of vigor due to inbreeding.

Ovulation--Release of the female germ cell (egg) by the ovary. Cows usually ovulate several hours (up to 15 hours) after the end of estrus or standing heat.

Parturition--The act of giving birth; calving.

Pedigree--A tabulation of names of ancestors, usually only those of the three to five closest generations.

Performance Data--The record of the individual animal for reproduction, production, and possibly carcass merit. Traits included would be birth, weaning and yearling weights, calving ease, calving interval, milk production, etc.

Performance Pedigree--A pedigree that includes performance records of ancestors, half and full sibs, and progeny in addition to the usual pedigree information. Also, the performance information is systematically combined to list estimated breeding values on the pedigrees by some breed associations.

Performance Test. In a performance test, phenotypic values for economically important traits are recorded on animals that have been managed as uniformly as possible, such that performance records will reflect transmissible genetic merit as accurately as possible.

Performance Testing--The systematic collection of comparative production information for use in decision making to improve efficiency and profitability of beef production. Differences in performance among cattle must be utilized in decision making for performance testing to be beneficial. The most useful performance records for management, selection, and promotion decisions will vary among purebred breeders and for purebred breeders compared with commercial cattle producers.

Phenotype--The visible or measurable expression of a

character; for example, weaning weight, postweaning gain, reproduction, etc. Phenotype is influenced by genotype and environment.

Phenotypic Correlations--Correlations between two traits caused by both genetic and environmental factors influencing both traits.

Phenotypic Selection -- Phenotypic selection occurs when individuals are selected to become the next generation of parents based upon their phenotypic merit for a particular trait or traits. Because "like tends to beget like", selection of phenotypically superior parents should increase progeny merit for the selected trait.

Planned Matings -- Planned matings occur when the cattle breeder chooses to mate a particular male with a particular female in an attempt to achieve a desired result. Crossbreeding is a planned mating, for example, when practiced in an attempt to benefit from heterosis. See also random mating.

Polled--Naturally hornless cattle. Having no horns or scurs.Planned matings. Planned matings occur when the cattle breeder chooses to mate a particular male with a particular female in an attempt to achieve a desired result.

Pounds of retail cuts per day of age--A measure of cutability and growth combined, it is calculated as follows: cutability times carcass weight divided by age in days. Also, it is reported as lean weight per day of age (LWDA) by some associations.

Possible change--The variation (either plus or minus) that is possible for each expected progeny difference (EPD). This measurement of error in prediction or estimation of EPD decreases as the number of offspring per sire increases.

Prepotent-The ability of a parent to transmit its characteristics on its offspring so that they resemble that parent, or each other, more than usual. Homozygous dominant individuals are prepotent. Also, inbred cattle tend to be more prepotent than outbred cattle.

Production Trait -- Production traits are those that directly influence cost or revenue from beef cattle production; growth rate, feed intake and carcass merit, for example.

Progeny records--The average, comparative performance of the progeny of sires and dams.

Progeny testing--Evaluating the genotype of an individual by a study of its progeny records.

Puberty--The age at which the reproductive organs become functionally operative and secondary sex characteristics begin to develop.

Purebred--An animal of known ancestry within a recognized breed that is eligible for registry in the official herdbook of that breed.

Qualitative traits-Those traits in which there is a sharp distinction between phenotypes, such as black and white or polled and horned. Usually, only one or few pairs of genes are involved in the expression of qualitative traits.

Quantitative trait--Those traits in which there is no sharp distinction between phenotypes, with a gradual variation from one phenotype to another, such as weaning weight. Usually, many gene pairs are involved, as well as environmental influences.

Random mating -- In random mating, the alternative to planned mating, males and females are mated without regard to their genetic relationship or to their phenotypic similarity. A system of mating where every female (cow and/or heifer) has an equal or random chance of being assigned to any bull used for breeding in a particular breeding season. Random mating may be required for accurate progeny tests.

Rate of genetic improvement-Rate of improvement per unit of time (year). The rate of improvement is dependent on: (1) heritability of traits considered; (2) selection differentials; (3) genetic correlations among traits considered; (4) generation interval in the herd; and (5) the number of traits for which selections are made.

Reach--See Selection differential.

Recessive gene--Recessive genes affect the phenotype only when present in a homozygous condition. Recessive genes must be received from both parents before the phenotype caused by the recessive genes can be observed.

Reference sire--A bull designated to be used as a benchmark in progeny testing other bulls (young sires). Progeny by reference sires in several herds enable comparisons to be made between bulls not producing progeny in the same herd(s).

Regression (regressed)-A measure of the relationship between two variables. The value of one trait can be predicted by knowing the value of the other variable. For example, easily obtained carcass traits (hot carcass weight, fat thickness, ribeye area, and percent of internal fat) are used to predict percent cutability. Likewise, breeding value estimates based on limited data are regressed back toward the population average to account for the imperfection of this relationship.

Rotational crossbreeding--Systems of crossing two or more breeds where the crossbred females are bred to bulls of the breed contributing the least genes to that female's genotype. Rotation systems maintain relatively high levels of heterosis and produce replacement heifers from within the system. Opportunity to select replacement heifers is greater for rotation systems than for other crossbreeding systems.

Scrotal circumference--A measure of testes size obtained by measuring the distance around the testicles in the scrotum with a circular tape. Related to semen producing capacity and age at puberty of female sibs and progeny.

Scurs--Horny tissue of rudimentary horns that are attached to the skin rather than the bony parts of the head.

Seedstock breeders--Producers of breeding stock for purebred and commercial breeders. Progressive seedstock breeders have comprehensive programs designed to produce an optimum or desirable combination of economical traits (genetic package) that will ultimately increase the profitability of commercial beef production.

Selection -- Causing or allowing certain individuals in a population to produce offspring in the next generation. Selection occurs when individuals of different genetic or phenotypic merit reproduce at different rates.

Relevant types of selection include:
Artificial selection. The livestock breeder decides which individuals will reproduce and for how long. Ideally, animals with highest predicted genetic merit for

economically important traits are chosen as parents, and those with the poorest estimated genetic merit are rejected or culled.

Natural selection. Whether an animal reproduces, and for how long, is determined by that animal's ability to cope with environmental challenges, rather than or in addition to breeder decisions.

Directional selection. Animals chosen to be parents are above (or below) the average of their contemporaries for the trait in question. The goal of directional selection is to improve phenotypic merit of the selected traits in progeny of the selected individuals.

Stabilizing selection. Those animals closest to average of their contemporaries are selected as parents, while animals that are either well above or well below average are discriminated against. The goal is to maintain the trait in question at its current level of expression. Stabilizing selection is appropriate for traits for which the optimum phenotype is an intermediate value.

Selection differential (reach)--The difference between the average for a trait in selected cattle and the average of the group from which they came. The expected response from selection for a trait is equal to selection differential times the heritability of the trait.

Selection Index . A formula that combines performance records from several traits or different measurements of the same trait into a single value for each animal. Selection indexes weigh the traits for their relative net economic importance and their heritabilities plus the genetic associations among the traits.

Selection Intensity -- Selection intensity is a numerical measure of a breeder's attempt to change a trait by choosing as parents those individuals with better than average estimated transmissible genetic merit for that trait. If all other things are equal, then higher selection intensity leads to higher selection response.

Selection Response -- Selection response is the amount by which the population mean for a trait is changed by the effects of selection, generally expressed per unit of time. See also correlated selection response.

Sibs--Brothers and sisters of an individual.

Sire summary--Published results of national sire evaluation

programs.

Stressor -- A stressor is any external challenge that causes an animal to initiate a physiological, behavioral and(or) immunological response to maintain or achieve its physical integrity and well-being. Examples include environmental temperatures outside the animal's inherent comfort zone, pathogenic organisms and dietary toxins.

Systems approach--An approach to evaluating alternative individuals, breeding programs, and selection schemes that involves assessment of these alternatives in terms of their net impact on all inputs and output in the production system. This approach specifically recognizes that intermediate optimum levels of performance in several traits may be more economically advantageous than maximum performance for any single trait.

Terminal sires--Sires used in a crossbreeding system where all their progeny, both male and female, are marketed. For example F1 crossbred dams could be bred to sires of a third breed and all calves marketed. Although this system allows maximum heterosis and complementary of breeds, replacement females must come from other herds.

Trait ratio--An expression of an animal's performance for a particular trait relative to the herd or contemporary group average.

USDA Yield Grade--Measurements of carcass cutability categorized into numerical categories with 1 being the leanest and 5 being the fattest. Yield grade and outability are based on the same four carcass traits.

Variance--Variance is a statistic that describes the variation we see in a trait. Without variation, no genetic progress is possible, since genetically superior animals would not be distinguishable from genetically inferior ones.

Weight per day of age (WDA)--Weight of an individual divided by days of age.

Index

About the Author

Morris Halliburton

Bells, Texas, USA

Been around cattle more than 75 years.

The information provided in this book is believed to be fairly accurate and up to date but as you peruse through the information you may want to remember that Morris probably qualifies as an "Old Timer" since his age is more than three Quarters of a Century. And then remember an often repeated definition of an "Old Timer" quoted many times as "a man who has had a lot of interesting experiences – some of them true."